RENEWAL OF THE TEACHER-SCHOLAR

Faculty Development in the Liberal Arts College

William C. Nelsen

Association of American Colleges

Renewal
of the
Teacher-Scholar

ISBN 0-911696-06-7

Dedicated to

Dr. Orville Zabel, Dr. Donald Wolfarth, and Dr. Allan Hauck, all genuine teacher-scholars, whom I encountered as a student in the early 1960s at Midland Lutheran College, Fremont, Nebraska, and who demonstrated that even at, perhaps especially at, relatively small colleges dedicated teacher-scholars can have lasting influence on the lives of students.

CONTENTS

PREFACE

Knowing the reading habits of persons in American higher education, I suspect that more administrators than faculty members will read this book. Such is not my intention, however.

The book arises from my serving in 1979 as the director of the Project on Faculty Development of the Association of American Colleges. During that year I traveled to twenty liberal arts colleges around the country and interviewed more than five hundred persons. At each campus I met with the president and academic dean, and sometimes several students, but most of my time was spent in conversation with faculty members. These normally very informative and lively sessions lead me to hope that the pages which follow would come to the attention of not only administrators, but also many faculty members, for two basic reasons.

First, this book contains not merely the thoughts of an academic administrator and researcher but also faculty themselves—their hopes and dreams, their discouragements and dissatisfactions, their praises and put-downs. The book is in large part a reporting of faculty perceptions of the possibilities for and the obstacles to the renewal of the teacher-scholar.

Second, faculty need to become more aware of the potential rich variety of opportunities for their own renewal. As I interviewed faculty, either individually or in groups, I was often appalled at their lack of knowledge concerning faculty development. To many, faculty development meant only the traditional programs of sabbaticals and travel to professional meetings. To others it was a catchy phrase referring only to improvement of teaching programs. Many faculty committees, assigned to encourage faculty renewal activities on their campuses, were struggling in the dark, often "reinventing the wheel," unaware of the great variety of programs and projects already underway and tested at other campuses. Yes, it is my hope that administrators will read, or at least skim, these pages, but my even greater hope is that they will encourage faculty to examine them as well, and that faculty will respond with their own ideas and goals for renewal.

The words in the title "Renewal of the Teacher-Scholar" are carefully chosen. Why the focus on the teacher-scholar? Much of the literature in the field of faculty development concentrates on one or another aspect of a faculty member's life—for example, the need to improve instruction, or more recently, alternative careers for faculty. Yet, the faculty member, especially in liberal arts colleges and universities, is called upon to pursue a variety of roles at the same time—teacher, adviser, scholar, contributor to campus and community life. The title at least suggests these wider simultaneous roles. Moreover, it appears that the ideal of the teacher-scholar must be re-examined. Is it still the model for the college and university faculty member? If so, how can colleges assist faculty in continually renewing themselves within that model?

The word "renewal" was chosen over two alternatives, "development" and "renewing." "Development of the teacher-scholar" would seem to

1

give emphasis to younger faculty or to persons who didn't yet quite fit the model. Renewal implies that all faculty should be in a continuing state of change and growth. "Renewing the teacher-scholar" would seem to imply that someone else is responsible for the faculty member's continuing development. To be sure, an atmosphere of support and encouragement is crucial, but in the long run faculty renewal is primarily self-renewal. It cannot be done *for* or *to* anyone else, only by the teacher-scholar himself or herself.

Many persons had a hand in the creation of this book. Thanks must go first to the administrators, faculty, and students of the twenty colleges which I visited in the spring of 1979: Austin, Bates, Beloit, Berea, Bowdoin, Colgate, Davidson, Earlham, Franklin and Marshall, Furman, Gettysburg, Haverford, Hope, Kenyon, Lawrence, Mt. Holyoke, Occidental, Pomona, St. Lawrence, and Trinity. Virtually everyone I met on these campuses was gracious and generous with his or her time. At each of the campuses I was assisted in the interviewing by a consultant knowledgeable about and experienced in faculty development. Altogether fifteen persons were utilized in this role, and they assisted admirably: Dr. George Allan, Dickinson College; Dr. Paula Brownlee, Hollins College; Dr. Richard Cantwell, Carleton College; Mrs. Gwen Clavadetscher, University of Puget Sound; Dr. Bradley Dewey, Franklin and Marshall College; the late Dr. J. Edward Dirks, University of California, Santa Cruz; Dr. Ann Ferren, American University; Dr. Donald Griffin, Rollins College; Dr. George Hazzard, AAC Project QUILL; Dr. Paul Lacey, Earlham College; Dr. Thomas Maher, Wichita State University: Dr. Glen Nelson, Luther College; Dr. E.C. Reckard, Centre College of Kentucky; Dr. Stephen Scholl, Kennedy College; and Dr. Al Smith, University of Florida.

A special word of appreciation must be said for several persons who made the AAC Project on Faculty Development possible. Dr. Mark Curtis, president of AAC and Dr. John Sawyer, president of the Andrew W. Mellon Foundation took leadership in creating the Project. The Mellon Foundation gave not only financial support but also personal encouragement through the continuing interest of Dr. Sawyer and Miss Claire List. Dr. Michael Siegel, associate director of the Project, gave invaluable assistance throughout the period of both research and writing. Dr. Eileen Kuhns, professor of higher education at Catholic University, provided many helpful insights into the design for research and interviewing. Mrs. Ellynn Crippin at AAC, Mrs. Jane Soli at St. Olaf, Verna Berg, Betty Egge, and several students at Augustana College worked hard and with great care, in typing and retyping the manuscript. Dr. Sidney A. Rand, former president of St. Olaf College and the college's Board of Regents were most generous and supportive in granting me a special leave to direct the Project.

I must thank an understanding and supportive family, for the year in which this book was researched was not an easy one. My wife of thirteen years, Nancy, died in September, 1979, after a struggle of more than three years with a brain tumor. She, and my children, Bill and Shawna, and our loyal family friend, Mrs. Ragna Evenson, gave support in countless ways. The writing was begun in late 1979 in Washington, D.C., continued during early 1980 after I returned to St. Olaf College in January, and completed in the year after I assumed the presidency at Augustana College in July, 1980. My attitude toward the final writing and editing were greatly aided by the thought of my new life with Margie, my bride since May, 1981 and her daughter, Sarah.

Several persons very generously agreed to give critical commentary and suggestions concerning the original manuscript: Jerry Gaff, Mark Curtis, and Michael Siegel. John Hager of AAC carefully oversaw the publication process. Thanks also to Carl Grupp of the Augustana College art department for the cover design.

Finally, the reader will note that I have chosen to use the first person frequently throughout this manuscript. This is to emphasize again that the ideas and concerns in this book arose from personal exchanges, usually in relatively informal settings, with faculty, administrators and students who were willing to share openly their concerns and hopes for the future of the teacher-scholar. Thus, whatever the book lacks in systematic survey analysis and formal reporting I hope has been replaced by an honest attempt at giving the reader a better feeling for the people who were the focus of these interviews.

Wiliam C. Nelsen
Augustana College
Sioux Falls, South Dakota
August, 1981

PART I

The Teacher-Scholar:
Renewal Of The Individual
And The Ideal

Chapter 1

The Teacher-Scholar Model: What Does It Mean Today?

> *Ideally the college professor would be a widely respected scholar excited about learning and capable of communicating this excitement to others, a teacher deeply concerned with the welfare of students and eager to have them learn and grow, one who teaches imaginatively both by books and by personal example, a demanding yet compassionate person who respects the moral worth of students and their potential for growth. While no one teacher is likely to realize all these attributes, the College must continually seek to recruit men and women who strive to do so to the greatest possible extent.* [1]

The above excerpt from the Davidson College Faculty Handbook (1979) states very well the model of the teacher-scholar. It has always been a prominent model in American higher education. Some might question the extent to which the model was present on particular campuses, but clearly it was there at the national level, exemplified perhaps best by the Danforth Foundation's E. Harris Harbison Award which went to ten outstanding teacher-scholars each year during the period 1962 to 1972.

But is the model still a viable one today? My interviews with faculty and administrators at twenty leading liberal arts colleges around the country revealed that the model is clearly tarnished and at some campuses close to falling apart. Faculty often perceived new tensions between teaching and scholarship and real uncertainty about the practicality of doing both well and being appreciated for even trying. This situation has led to tensions not only between "teaching" and "scholarship" but worse yet between "teachers" and "scholars" (with self-perceptions providing the categories). Faculty members during interviews would often put down another colleague for concentrating too much on teaching or vice versa on scholarship.

To a certain extent tensions between teaching and scholarship are normal and unavoidable. There is truth in Donald Light's assessment: "If research scholars teach better, it is due to their being smarter and more energetic rather than to their doing research. While much depends on what kind of research is being done and what courses are being taught, as well as who the individual is, most faculty feel they have two jobs competing for their time." [2]

But these tensions between scholarship and teaching can be overplayed so that the situation becomes harmful, even destructive, to both individual faculty members and college academic life generally. As one faculty member said: "I hate this false dichotomy between teaching and research. The active researcher around here always seems to get the reputation that he is not giving enough time to teaching." Likewise, other faculty were heard to say, "Sure he's a popular teacher, but he won't do our department much good. We need more researchers."

What has brought about this increased tension, this tarnishing of the teacher-scholar model? Interviews with faculty and administrators indicated a variety of causes.

Wider tensions in the profession itself may be responsible. Faculty often remarked about their perceptions of being "locked in" to a stagnant situation, their sense of being underpaid, their fear of staff reductions, the lack of enthusiasm among their colleagues. Some faculty remarked that seeing some of their colleagues engaged in collective bargaining had left them with a new source of tension—between a feeling that they ought to join the battle for more benefits and a distaste for the noneducational, nonscholarly goals of the process. One college president voiced concern for faculty when he described college teaching as "the depressed profession" for the next ten to fifteen years. These wider tensions have seemingly resulted in more "internal competition" among faculty—as "teachers" and "scholars" compete for scarce resources for their departments, slots for tenure, and funds for promotions and salary increases.

Another culprit may be what can be described as the "individualization" of the professoriate. The increased specialization of graduate school training plus the growth of departmentalization within colleges and universities have led faculty to operate within narrow confines. Faculty often spoke of a feeling of separation from their colleagues in other departments and many times within their own department. The result is what some faculty described as a "loss of colleagueship"—and an increase in suspicion as to what others "over there" are doing in both teaching and research.

The tension has been heightened by increased skepticism of the quality and value of some scholarly work. The academic machine has indeed been known to produce very narrow, sometimes not very meaningful publications. While many faculty may react negatively to scholarly activities of colleagues out of jealousy, defensiveness, or lack of understanding, their skepticism may not be entirely unfounded. As one faculty member put it, "One can achieve a great deal of status nationally without having a quality of mind."

A related source of tension is what some faculty called a false view of professionalism. To be professional in the minds of some faculty means directing all your time and energy to your discipline, your research, and your professional association. Some ask, where are the students in all of this? One faculty member pointed to this concern when he stated, "I don't feel I have to sacrifice 'professionalism' to get more involved with students."

But colleges themselves must shoulder a great deal of the blame for the blurring of the teacher-scholar model in two important ways—by their lack of clear guidelines for faculty evaluation and by the way in which faculty development programs have been constructed. Not all colleges have such clear statements of "preferred faculty" as the Davidson one at the beginning of this chapter, and even on many campuses which do, actual practices belie the statements. Faculty often complained of the confusion in signals, judging from who was getting promoted and who wasn't, trying to figure out what importance was attached to professional contributions and to teaching evaluations by colleagues, department chairpersons, deans, and presidents. At one campus, an administrator stressed, "We have given even greater emphasis to *scholarship* through our new program of small research grants to faculty." A faculty gathering on the same campus revealed a different perception: "There seems to be a lot of stress on *teaching* from the administration here. You better darn well get a good student evaluation and get good enrollments if you want rewards around here." At another campus faculty members were calling for a special series of meetings to clarify the expectations of the college for them as teachers and scholars. This lack of clear signals may be acceptable to some faculty, but it is troublesome to most—especially to younger faculty, who, in facing difficult tenure decisions hear colleagues and administrators speaking in an array of conflicting voices.

Similarly, colleges may have unwittingly damaged the teacher-scholar model by the way in which they have structured programs of faculty renewal. Instructional development centers created at larger universities have, in certain instances, given attention only to teaching improvement, apart from the scholarly and research concerns of faculty. Even relatively smaller colleges have fostered programs which separated the roles of faculty in some confusing ways. For example, one campus had two separate faculty committees to oversee college grants for faculty—a research council and a faculty development council—which seemed to suggest that improvement in research opportunities was not an important part of faculty development. Colleges have also created faculty development programs which provided opportunities for renewal of faculty only as individuals, thereby unintentionally diminishing group interaction and colleagueship and further encouraging the "individualization of the professoriate."

Is the teacher-scholar model still viable? Can the model itself be renewed? There is little doubt in my mind that it is still a valid concept and an important ideal to keep before us. Of course, individual faculty members will always emphasize teaching and scholarship in varying degrees, but is there really any doubt that a faculty member ought to be both teacher and scholar—at least in the broad sense?

In his Prologue to the *Canterbury Tales* Chaucer concludes the description of the Clerk of Oxford with the words, "and gladly would he learn and gladly teach." Can a faculty member really be a good teacher unless he continues to take seriously (and gladly) his own *learning*—his scholarly development? For a while, perhaps, but indefinitely, no. One college president (an experienced faculty member himself) described the following scenario of many older faculty: "They start out being popular with students; they depend on students for their 'teaching rewards.' But they are engaged in no sustained research or intellectual growth. Soon students turn to other faculty, as younger, more active persons arrive on the campus. The more senior, nonproductive faculty lose enthusiasm for their work, become frustrated, and struggle cheerlessly through their teaching assignments."

Another faculty member described the importance of continuing scholarly development in this way: "You simply can't be an effective teacher unless you are up to what's going on. A teacher needs to be excited about what he's doing. The active scholar creates a satisfying atmosphere for the students, because they know they are not going to a second-rate institution."

The assumption is not being made here that good scholarship automatically produces good teaching. Some faculty do support this assumption, but most are unwilling to do so because they have seen too many examples of outstanding scholars who have not responded to changes among students or recognized their own weakness in teaching and communicating their knowledge. The question is always raised however, can individual scholars ever really improve in teaching? Isn't teaching too much a part of our personalities? Interviews with faculty indicated that indeed some faculty may change their teaching style, approach, and effectiveness very little throughout their academic lives. But this is not true for all. As the later chapters on instructional development indicate, there are many successful instances of campus programs for teaching improvement and personal testimonies that indicated that change is possible.

The model of the teacher-scholar may be gone forever in certain types of higher educational institutions—where teaching or scholarship is so heavily emphasized to the detriment of the other—but surely in those places where it has traditionally been revered, especially the undergraduate liberal arts programs of our colleges and universities, we cannot and must not let this important model be lost.

Colleges cannot eliminate all the forces that have recently plagued the teacher-scholar. Some are economic, social, and political forces which must be dealt with at more comprehensive levels. But colleges can renew and protect the teacher-scholar in many crucial ways. They can change their reward structures, their evaluation systems, their curriculum to encourage improvement of *both* teaching and scholarship. They can, through corporate faculty activity, work against the individualization of the professoriate; they can by their words and deeds, demonstrate a broader approach to professionalism; they can provide clearer signals and expectations for faculty to encourage high-quality scholarship *and* teaching. Perhaps most importantly they can build essential faculty renewal programs that do not falsely sever teaching and scholarship but instead seek to integrate these in both the program of the college and the professional lives of individual faculty. This book reports on the stimulating and exciting ways in which some colleges have already begun this task and makes suggestions for additional ways these and other colleges can seek to renew the teacher-scholar.

---

[1]Davidson College Faculty Handbook, draft report, 1979.
[2]Donald Light, Jr., "Thinking about Faculty," *Daedulus* 103 (Fall, 1974), p. 258.

Chapter 2

Continuing Renewal: Institutional Need and Individual Incentive

In the course of an interview with one college president, he remarked: "One of my greatest responsibilities—and constant worries—is delivering an exciting and excited faculty member to a group of relatively good students." In that statement he was trying to summarize what he saw as central to quality education at his campus. Some colleges may differ as to the importance of having "relatively good students" since many see their mission as working with students of differing abilities, but surely no college, whether highly selective or very open in its admissions policy, could disclaim the importance of having faculty members who are excited about what they are doing and possess the ability, knowledge, and acquired sensitivity to stimulate student learning.

But providing continually stimulating and motivated faculty members to students is a major charge, for faculty personnel, like anyone else, have the proven ability to become less exciting and excited, to stop growing and renewing themselves. For teacher-scholars in colleges and universities this propensity toward stagnation has always been a danger, but as indicated in the previous chapter the pressures today seem more imposing than in previous years and the need for attention to renewal even more critical.

Why is there need for so great an emphasis on renewal at this time? A number of factors have emerged in recent years which have caused us to focus on faculty renewal more intensively than previously.

As the Group for Human Development in Higher Education highlighted in their 1974 publication, *Faculty Development in a Time of Retrenchment*, we were entering a time of decreased mobility for faculty as enrollments declined and fewer slots became available for junior faculty. Administrators and faculty themselves began to voice real concern about whether new ideas and curricular changes could be forthcoming in relatively stable faculties. One faculty member in an interview stated this concern well when he said, "If we can't get *new* people, we must at least have *renewed* people."

But the emerging problems of the 1970s and expectations of the 1980s have brought forth an even more troublesome reason for this focus on renewal. The difficulties of faculty adapting to "steady-state," retrenchment, high inflation rates and lower-than-desired salary increases, and the isolationist and competitive atmosphere described in the previous chapter have led to a feeling of malaise and even despair among many faculty. One administrator voiced the fear that these negative feelings might cause colleges to "turn inward upon ourselves" just at a time when leadership by the academy in our society was vitally needed. Programs of renewal are needed to encourage among faculty a new sense of vitality, enthusiasm, and even self-worth.

We are learning that renewal is crucial for faculty at all stages of their careers. The stable and potentially declining enrollment situation plus the relatively high percentage of tenured faculty in our institutions have caused us to focus special attention on senior and "mid-career" faculty. For many of these faculty adaptations to new student clientele, higher expectations, and the continuing knowledge explosion is not easy. Most difficult perhaps is getting many senior faculty to be open and honest in recognizing their own need for renewal. As one college president said in frustration, "It's a devastating thing to acknowledge; how many faculty who are in this mid-career position will admit their own needs?" Still, no matter how difficult, renewal for senior faculty is crucial for a variety of reasons. Immediately we think of renewal in relation to the key teacher-scholar roles—the need for revitalized teaching and continuing scholarly pursuits. Yet, just as important for senior faculty is their role as model for younger faculty. In most colleges, according to both faculty perceptions and administrative acknowledgement, standards and expectations for faculty have risen in recent years. Many senior faculty were tenured and received promotions under a different set of requirements. Thus, senior faculty are often put in the difficult position of urging junior faculty to publish as soon as possible and experiment in their teaching while finding it difficult to do so themselves. This situation often causes frustration for senior faculty and resentment from junior faculty. Senior faculty are no longer looked to as mentors and models. Renewal programs for senior faculty are needed to help them return to their proper status.

Younger faculty also need renewal programs as soon as they begin their post-doctorate careers. Most graduate school programs prepare persons quite well for research within their disciplines—or at least a part of their disciplines—but usually quite poorly for teaching a variety of subjects in an undergraduate program. Thus, it is up to the college itself to encourage junior faculty to move beyond the Ph.D. dissertation in scholarly pursuits, to understand and experiment with a variety of approaches to teaching, and to broaden intellectual horizons for the sake of both their own teaching and the college's wider curricular goals. Also, this immediate immersion into faculty development activities can help the younger faculty member realize that the liberal arts ideal of learning for life is meant not only for students but also for faculty. One faculty member in an interview expressed the same belief as follows: "The best type of faculty development is preventative. It's too hard to bring deadwood back to life."

In a related manner, an active faculty development program can help a college to recruit outstanding young faculty interested in continuing growth as teachers and scholars. One active young faculty member emphasized this when he reported: "When I visited this campus, I quickly learned that the college was committed to faculty renewal and long-term career development. That helped me to decide to come to this place."

Some colleges have already experienced faculty and staff retrenchment as a result of enrollment decline and others are likely to do so in the coming decade. What then is the place of faculty renewal? Interviews on campuses which had wrestled with the problem of retrenchment revealed that renewal was sometimes different in nature but not in its importance. In a period of declining staff the emphasis for some faculty may shift from personal growth to preparation for curricular readjustment as faculty are called upon to fill in the gaps. For all faculty a renewal program which continues during times of retrenchment can be an important factor in preventing morale from dropping too low.

But perhaps the most important reason for maintaining an active renewal program is that without it both individuals and the college in which they serve can too quickly lose their sense of life and liveliness. In his book *Self-Renewal*, John Gardner forcefully expresses this important principle: "The ever-renewing organization (or society) is not one which is convinced that it enjoys eternal youth. It knows that it is forever growing old and must do something about it. It knows that it is always producing deadwood and must, for that reason, attend to its seedbeds. The seedlings are new ideas, new ways of doing things, new approaches."[1]

Gardner is also one who believes that self-renewal is possible: "As for self-renewal, we know that men and women need not fall into a stupor of mind and spirit by the time they are middle-aged. They need not relinquish as early as they do the resilience of youth and the capacity to learn and grow. Self-renewal is possible."[2]

But for most persons self-renewal does not come easily or automatically. One faculty member, who had spent a great amount of time counseling faculty colleagues, summarized the difficulty: "Professional reeducation is a major undertaking. You don't go through Ph.D., postdoc, teaching acclimatization, and then change easily."

It is important to recognize that not all faculty are the same. Some faculty are continually ready for self-renewal and high productivity, others demonstrate varying degrees of readiness. In the opinion of the academic dean at one of the twenty campuses, faculty can be divided into three major groups in relation to the question of continuing faculty development: 1) those productive faculty who will renew themselves and produce even with very little aid and encouragement; 2) those who provide minimal output no matter what the incentives; and 3) a fairly large group that could go either way, who require some stimulation and assistance and who often will respond.

Granted that a number of faculty often need and will respond to incentives, the next question becomes, what incentives work best? Interviews with faculty on this matter revealed that there is no single answer.

Rewards obviously make a difference to a great many faculty. Promotion or merit pay which links active faculty development with salary increase is the most direct form of reward. But faculty indicated that other types of rewards are just as important. Simple acknowledgement—if not praise—from an administrator or a faculty colleague can be a major incentive toward continuing renewal. Faculty often expressed to me the significance in their lives of knowing that someone else at least was aware of, and hopefully cared about, what they were doing in both teaching and scholarship.

Even where personal salary increase does not result, most colleges with faculty development programs provide some extra funds for specific projects in research or course development. Some thoughtful administrators and faculty were correct in voicing concern about the long-term consequences of always dangling money in front of faculty to encourage research, writing, or any kind of renewal activities. They ask: "Doesn't this run the risk of faculty always expecting 'extra' for faculty development work?"

While this danger is very real, there are some important counter-reasons that indicate the current importance of additional funds for faculty development. First, travel, research, and equipment expenses are often considerable—usually beyond faculty members' personal budgets or the meager help they might obtain from departmental budgets. Second, providing stipends for faculty engaged in special kinds of renewal in place of their teaching summer school or taking on a "moonlighting" position is a legitimate means of encouraging faculty to use their time for the benefit of the college. Third, it is hard for a college to show its commitment to faculty renewal apart from financial appropriations. At the same time, the faculty member in accepting the funds also makes a commitment to carry out the project. As one key member of a faculty development committee remarked, "We often need something that gives a faculty member a form of commitment. Money is one form of commitment." Fourth, providing funds for stipends or project expenses also allows for greater accountability. The faculty member must be accountable for the use of time and money provided by the grant from the college.

Providing an award or grant for a teacher-scholar to pursue research or teaching improvement does more than simply allow him or her to meet the required expenses. It is also an important sign of recognition, a sign which many faculty seldom receive because of the intense competition for awards from national funding agencies. One college president, referring to a mid-career faculty member who had received a grant from the college's faculty development funds for the first time, observed: "He has not yet started his project, but already he stands a little taller. He speaks with a little more assurance."

However, time and again during interviews faculty members indicated in various ways that the greatest incentive for renewal was a changed *total environment* on campus—an environment where standards, rewards, and expectations clearly called for continuing renewal. John Gardner, in discussing organizational renewal, makes the same point: "The development of abilities is at least in part a dialogue between the individual and his environment. If he has it to give and the environment demands it, the ability will develop."[3] On many campuses which had been engaged in active renewal programs, one major, lasting impact was the raising of standards and expectations. As a leading faculty member at one campus observed: "The faculty here now has a higher self-expectation for self-development."

Self-renewal *is* possible—and it *is* being carried out on many campuses. Surprisingly, interviews in the AAC Project on Faculty Development revealed that the whole concept of "faculty development" was also generally accepted. One faculty member remarked a bit sarcastically, "First, the name of the game was publish or perish, then obtain a grant or perish, now its develop or perish!" But for most faculty the term "faculty development" had merely become part of the educational world and conjured up more positive than negative reactions. This was especially the case where faculty had played an important role in planning and overseeing the development program. A faculty member at one campus remarked: "The term seems to generate no negative response here, perhaps because it has been associated with a project where faculty have real influence and support for their initiatives."

While faculty development was generally accepted, it was not always conceived by faculty in the same way. Unfortunately on some campuses the conception was very narrow. At one campus it still meant primarily "take a sabbatical." On several other campuses it meant sabbaticals, plus travel to professional meetings. At a few campuses the term meant something quite different. For example, it often aroused suspicions of new "teaching gimmicks." Some persons who operate faculty development centers on larger campuses which focus only on teaching pedagogy are partially to blame for this narrow conception. One director of such a center referred to "the emerging field of faculty development" as designating *only* "instructional development, teaching improvement, etc."

Thus, one of the major tasks for colleges undertaking faculty renewal programs is to educate themselves and their faculties concerning the variety of renewal possibilities in *both teaching and scholarship.* Faculty (and many administrators) were often unaware of the rich possibilities for renewal which had already been undertaken at other colleges.

In the AAC Project, we conceived of faculty development as encompassing four specific areas—professional development (scholarship, improved research skills, broadening of scholarly areas); instructional development (pedagogy, improved teaching skills, learning of new techniques); curricular change (preparation for new courses, significant changes in current offerings, development of interdisciplinary courses); and organizational change (enhancing faculty renewal through alterations in committee systems, reward structures, new campus-wide goals). The next section of this volume examines important issues in renewing the teacher-scholar through these four basic approaches, as we focus first on "the scholar," then "the teacher," then the content of teaching, and finally the setting.

If colleges recognize that faculty renewal is indeed possible and that programs and incentives should be broadly conceived to meet a variety of needs for their faculty, we will have come a long way not only in renewing individual teacher-scholars, but also in rebuilding the model of the teacher-scholar.

---

[1] John W. Gardner, *Self-Renewal: The Individual and the Innovative Society* (New York: Harper & Row, 1965), p. 68.
[2] *Ibid*, p. xiii
[3] *Ibid*, p. 11.

PART II

Approaches To Renewal Of The Teacher-Scholar

Chapter 3

Renewing the Teacher as Scholar

If a faculty member is to renew himself or herself as a teacher-scholar, continuing professional development is essential. What do we mean by "professional development" in this context?

At the heart of professional development is scholarship. But scholarship must not be viewed too narrowly. Often it is perceived as meaning only research and publication. As emphasized in the first chapter, pursuing research into valuable areas and expressing thoughts carefully in written form are very important in the ongoing renewal of the mind. But a lively mind can also be maintained in other ways—scholarly study related directly to course preparation, presenting ideas and formal papers to colleagues either on-campus or in professional meetings, taking leadership in professional associations, thinking creatively as a consultant for public groups or agencies. Moreover, professional development takes on different forms depending on one's discipline; for some writing is the chief manifestation of scholarly renewal, but for others it is painting, sculpturing, musical performance, theatrical production, speaking and debating, or placing a well-coached team on the field. Scholarship in essence means continuing to develop your own abilities and at some point placing your work, your preparation, your results in public view for others to see and evaluate. The faculty member, of course, always has his or her students as a critical public audience, but the true teacher-scholar will seek critical audiences beyond the classroom as well.

Approaches to Professional Development. How can colleges encourage continuing professional development among their faculties? Visits to campuses in the AAC Project on Faculty Development revealed that there are a variety of important issues to consider.

It is essential that a college have funds specifically designated for professional renewal of faculty. As stressed earlier, this "professional development fund" need not be narrowly conceived. At Earlham College, for example, the Professional Development Fund includes the following areas for eligible projects: pursuing research and scholarship, preparing interdisciplinary courses, initiating various curricular programs, improving skills, developing a specific competence, improving a scholarly area, and facilitating long-range growth plans.

Funds are essential to allow faculty to overcome partially the financial difficulties of pursuing research and study in an inflationary economy. One faculty member, near the top of the pay scale at his college voiced this problem as follows: "Speaking as a humanist, a person not independently wealthy, and at mid-career, can I sustain economically a career at this college? In order to pursue professional development I need funds for summer study and research because as a humanist I am not able ordinarily to obtain additional salary support elsewhere by consulting. Travel for research is virtually impossible without extra support; so is taking a full-year sabbatical." Most faculty are simply not frequently able to take on certain kinds of study and research, using only their own resources.

The mere existence of a professional development fund is an important stimulus to renewal in the perception of many faculty. "Professional development monies are an invitation to creative thinking," remarked one faculty member. A formal faculty development fund provides "a lack of excuses not to pursue scholarly work," observed another person. Perhaps the most telling remark came from a faculty member who was asked to judge the effect of the professional development fund on his campus. His reply: "It is difficult to judge impact because projects are varied and scattered, but it is psychologically very important to me just to know that it's there."

Funds for professional growth allow a faculty member to think beyond his or her immediate setting to broader issues of the profession. When asked about the impact of faculty development funds on his campus, one faculty member was quick to point out that "due to grant monies on campus I was able to do more in my profession; I have been in touch much more with persons in my profession outside the campus."

A formal professional development fund, in addition to providing financial support for specific faculty renewal efforts, may have other important spin-offs. For example, in connection with internal competition for funds, faculty often spoke of the value in learning how to write better grant proposals (especially in the humanities where faculty have had less experience in doing this). Also, several campus faculty development leaders observed that the availability of funds prompted new projects which, although they did not receive funding in the on-campus competition, were carried out nevertheless, often by faculty finding funds elsewhere.

In sum, the existence of professional development funds on campus is extremely helpful not only for meeting financial needs but also for stimulating creative thinking. A faculty member at a college with an active renewal fund expressed this conclusion in a similar way: "The funds have enabled a number of faculty here to do things that they *might* not have done and some people to do things they *could* not have done."

The most popular usage of professional development funds on the campuses visited is the awarding of competitive grants to individuals for research, travel, or study. While there are certain dangers to too much emphasis on individually oriented approaches to renewal (See Chapter 11), there is no doubt about the potential value of a well-administered program of individual grants. The summer faculty research grants at Hope College in Holland, Michigan, provide an excellent example of such a program. One interviewer at that campus judged that these grants had brought about "a significant increase in scholarly activity." The faculty had become involved much more extensively in writing grant proposals, publishing articles and books and conducting various types of scholarly activities. In 1978-79, fifty percent of the faculty applied for summer research grants, and approximately seventy-five percent had applied for a summer grant during the four years of the formal program. Hope faculty revealed the positive impact of the program in various comments: "I believe that these grants have increased both the competence and the confidence of many faculty." "The college is now much more lively during the summer months." "Some of our faculty who were very ready to relax have now been taking on something new." At another college which also had an active individual grant program, one faculty member summarized its psychological importance as follows: "These grants in effect say to us, 'Your life has a larger meaning than just teaching and meeting classes.'"

Providing released time to a faculty member for study or research is another common approach to professional renewal. Reducing the faculty member's load by one or two courses is often a relatively easy way to provide additional time for scholarly work. However, interviews with faculty revealed that there are some risks involved. The "released time" can quickly be filled with college activities other than scholarship. The costs of replacing a faculty member with part-time help are usually higher than providing a summer stipend. If too many faculty members in a particular department are granted released time, the teaching and curriculum of the department can be damaged—to the detriment of both the college and the students. At other times a certain amount of released time can be effectively managed. The important question must be: What are the pay-offs for both individual faculty and the college in the long run?

Another especially appropriate approach to professional renewal in the liberal arts college is faculty-student research grants. With the utilization of students for research assistance, funding can be stretched further. The research experience is helpful not only to the scholarly contribution of the faculty member but also to the development of research skills for the student. Wherever we encountered this approach to renewal, appreciation was voiced by both faculty and students.

Consistently revealed in the interviews with faculty on the twenty campuses was their lack of awareness of issues, events, and practices at other colleges. Faculty can become very parochial, especially during this period of decreased mobility. One way often suggested to counter this situation is faculty exchange. Several faculty who had participated in an exchange with a colleague at another college articulated a number of important professional outcomes including: contributing new perspectives to the host institution; gaining different perspectives of one's own college; revising courses to meet different departmental and student needs; having more time as a result of being out of committee work for a year; and enjoying a different environment for both professional and personal reasons. But the expressed desire for more faculty exchange has never been matched by implementation of the idea. Except where two faculty members in the same discipline at different colleges are personally acquainted and both have administrative support, faculty exchanges are difficult to arrange. A more aggressive role by administrators, probably working through a consortial arrangement, is needed to make exchanges occur more frequently.

Faculty could also enlarge their professional perspectives a great deal via brief visits to other campuses. At one campus as a part of the faculty development program faculty spent several days exchanging ideas with colleagues at other institutions. They recognized that it was one thing to talk with faculty from other colleges at a professional meeting in a large city hotel and quite another to view at first hand their setting for teaching and scholarship. Colleges would do well to consider spending more funds on faculty travel to other colleges, perhaps even in place of some of the discipline-oriented professional meetings.

In order to facilitate professional renewal, colleges have also begun to examine ways in which the traditional sabbatical program can be adjusted. The regular program of a half-year at full pay or a full year at half pay following six years of teaching is still the most widely used, but because of budgetary pressures for the college and the financial difficulty for faculty arranging a full year away, alternatives are being tried. For example, Colgate University has an accelerated leave program whereby a faculty member, in order to carry out a stated plan of research, can get a term off by teaching three extra courses (no more than one extra course per year) as an overload. Carleton College has a similar accelerated leave program. Several colleges have gone the direction of shorter-term, yet more frequent leaves, since it is easier—and less expensive—to not replace faculty who are on leave for a single term. Colgate has also initiated a junior faculty leave program which provides leaves for non-tenured faculty after three or four years. Its purpose is to encourage beginning scholars to move beyond their dissertation topics—to get in the habit early of "finishing a project in one area and restarting another."

Strategies for Spending Professional Development Funds Effectively. Once a college has obtained outside funds or budgeted some of its own resources for professional development, it must wrestle with several key questions of strategy. Should the fund be wide open or targeted at certain needs or groups? Should some funds be reserved to meet unexpected needs and requests?

The targeted approach to using renewal funds has several advantages. A faculty committee can call for proposals designed to bring about change in specific areas. A certain age group of faculty might also be encouraged in its renewal. For example, one college had a program specifically aimed at "mid-career" faculty. At certain times renewal for a certain area or group may be extremely important to the college. At other times a competition for professional renewal funds open to all faculty may work best. This strategy allows a variety of individual needs to be met.

To assist faculty in meeting immediate needs and opportunities several colleges have established a "Deans Discretionary Fund" or something similar. This allows the dean not only to respond to requests for unforeseen faculty opportunities, but also to encourage some of the less aggressive faculty with carefully aimed monetary support.

The issues of supporting new projects vs. those already started and of assisting faculty just beginning vs. those with a proven track record are not easy ones. Some college faculty development committees are quite adamant in funding only those faculty who can point to specific accomplishments. Concerning one college with a stated philosophy that "good money should go to already productive people" one of the interviewers commented: "Faculty in real need of renewal have been abandoned; the scholarly 'stars' are being encouraged and their morale is thus heightened. This strategy is probably a good thing for the nine or ten faculty each year who are winners but it is clearly discouraging to some of those faculty who, as a result, will never apply, let alone win, those awards." The president at the same college admitted his doubts about their current strategy: "I'm a little skeptical. Will the same persons get grants time and time again? Are we simply making it easier for those who already get support? What about those who need a resurgence of interest?"

At another campus the faculty development committee took the opposite point of view. They decided that they would give priority to new projects and recognized that this would involve some risks. A sensible policy would seem to be to not exclude systematically any group—to recognize that certain faculty with established scholarly records need support and yet to leave room to assist the beginning scholar and the more reluctant senior faculty in need of renewal. This will mean, as several colleges have discovered, balancing wide-open competition with subtle pressure by the dean or faculty leaders to encourage less aggressive faculty.

Faculty Growth Planning. In order to get faculty members to think comprehensively about their continuing professional development several colleges have initiated programs of long-term faculty growth planning. Operating under several names—faculty growth contracts, career development plans, faculty growth plans—the basic idea is to get faculty to think about their professional goals and plans for renewal over a three-to-five year span. In the process of developing his or her plan, the faculty member usually takes into account self-evaluation or evaluations from other sources, consults with several faculty colleagues and administrators, and finally puts in writing specific goals and means for achieving those goals. At certain colleges the plan must be approved by a committee or an administrator. Liberal arts colleges with formal faculty growth planning include Gordon College, Furman University, St. Olaf

25

College and Austin College.

How have faculty reacted to the idea of growth planning? While there is ordinarily great skepticism among faculty who have not tried to develop a growth plan, among participants there was usually strong support for the idea. At Furman University, for example, where growth planning has been focused on the "mid-career" group, faculty reactions included the following: "It helped to crystallize my thinking instead of my floundering around in a fuzzy future." "It forced me to think beyond immediate ideas for which funding was available." "It was an agonizing process, but I believe it was worth it."

At Austin College their "career development planning" arose from the faculty and administration looking at possible alternatives to tenure. They decided to keep the tenure system, but they added the provision that tenure brought with it the ongoing responsibility for participating in career development planning. Failure to do so could be grounds for dismissal. Moreover, a faculty member at Austin cannot be considered for tenure, promotion, or sabbatical unless he or she has a career development plan approved by the appropriate faculty and administrative officers. One faculty member at Austin observed that career planning "keeps the tenured faculty conscious of where they are going." Another observed that many faculty had found the planning experience to be "painful but very helpful."

The term "career development plan" is used quite deliberately at Austin. That is, the emphasis is not merely on the next few years but on one's long-term professional career. As a result of several faculty being forced to look long-range, there was exploration of alternative careers both within and outside the academy. In at least one case a faculty member resigned to pursue another career, directly as a result of attempting a career development plan.

There is no hidden magic in writing faculty growth or career development plans. No real changes may result for many faculty, but for others the process itself may be extremely important. For the sake of both individual and institutional renewal, colleges should look seriously at instituting formal growth planning.

The Climate for Professional Renewal. The possibilities for professional renewal programs for the teacher-scholar are almost endless. This chapter has suggested only a limited number that seem to have been effective at several campuses. Other programs in professional development are described briefly in the appendix.

Each college should decide what particular approach is best for its faculty, but no matter what approach is used the aim must be to create a climate on campus wherein professional growth for the teacher-scholar is both expected and supported. This change of climate was observed at several of the colleges in the AAC project. At one campus with an active program of grants for summer study and research, one interviewer reported: "The program has encouraged a number of faculty to get involved who were previously on the sidelines. The climate and expectations for faculty development have definitely improved. Even non-participants were strongly supportive and observed positive results."

At another campus one of the interviewers described the impact of the faculty development program as follows: "It has been the enabling legislation that permitted the university to uphold standards of faculty scholarship, much more than was previously possible. That is, money was available to demonstrate that good people with good ideas would be funded and that good teaching had to be backed up with good scholarship." Renewal of the teacher-scholar cannot be accomplished without a supportive climate for professional renewal.

Chapter 4

The Call for a "New Scholarship"

It has been documented time and again that only a relatively small percentage of faculty in American colleges and universities publish on a regular basis. According to Donald Light, "If the professional is the person who steadily produces scholarly works, about twenty percent of the faculty belong to the academic profession."[1] In the face of this fact Light proposes a "new model for excellence" for undergraduate teachers, emphasizing teaching. There is clearly a need to reward good teaching much more than we have, but, if one believes that continuing scholarly growth is essential to good teaching, Light's model must be expanded. Should eighty percent of the faculty not be encouraged to put their ideas on paper, to test their thoughts on certain issues not only with their students but also with their peers? Yet if they did, would the present world of publishing be able to accommodate more articles, books, and papers? Probably not. Thus, this call for a "new scholarship."

It is not easy for college faculty—especially undergraduate teachers—to pursue scholarship in the traditional sense. Teaching loads often dictate against it, and when these are overcome, either by hard work or some released time (or both), they face real difficulties in getting their work published. Publishing costs have risen substantially, forcing many journals to cut back production, while competition has increased with the growth of faculty size in the 1950s, 1960s, and early 1970s.

Of course a few faculty in liberal arts colleges are able to get their works published by recognized journals and publishing houses. But many either give up or are forced into often fairly narrow areas where publication in more specialized journals seems possible. Almost every discipline has within it a small coterie of people attracted to a particular subject who begin a journal—sometimes very useful, but often not very helpful or relevant to the world of the undergraduate liberal arts professor.

This criticism of some specialized journals must be understood carefully, for it is aimed primarily at the humanities, arts and social sciences and less at the natural sciences. One can understand and appreciate a natural scientist working in a fairly narrow area, for what may seem to be on the fringe may actually produce an important discovery at the heart of his or her discipline. But the humanities and arts suffer if they pursue such a course, leading them away from the tradtional contributions they have made (and need to make now more than ever) in discussing larger questions of life's meaning and values. Likewise, the social sciences have been criticized for often being preoccupied with methodology at the expense of tackling more meaningful questions for society for which precise methodology may never be discovered.

The present situation is troublesome for both senior and junior faculty. Many senior faculty have little interest in pursuing publication, either because they perceive the competition to be too stiff or they have little interest in pursuing overly narrow topics. In recent years this lack of scholarly production by senior faculty has led to real resentment by junior faculty who face higher standards for scholarly work for reappointment and tenure. As one bright, young faculty member remarked during an interview, "Most senior faculty around here don't publish, and yet we are expected to. This produces lots of bitter feeling."

For junior faculty the present situation creates an unhealthy, frustrating division between teaching and scholarship. Their scholarship often forces them into narrow pursuits just at the time when they are trying to learn to teach the central concerns of their disciplines. One senior faculty member, very concerned about younger faculty being pressured to publish too soon, observed: "Younger faculty are forced into peripheral commitments rather than central concerns in the discipline. The result is that good people are being ruined. The situation is defeating of not only good teaching but also good scholarship in the long run."

Once again, colleges have sometimes added to the problem by the way in which they have structured faculty development programs. At the campuses we visited many small grants had been awarded to junior faculty to pursue highly specialized research. One academic dean admitted, "We may be encouraging some kinds of scholarship that are not very useful in the liberal arts college, or indeed anywhere!"

For those faculty, junior or senior, wishing to move outside their disciplines and pursue interdisciplinary scholarly study and writing, the problems become even more acute. While a number of new interdisciplinary journals have arisen in recent years, they are not yet significant enough in quantity nor reputation in the minds of many. Also, a suspicious eyebrow is often raised by departmental colleagues when a faculty member ventures into interdisciplinary work. Commented one faculty member: "I feel caught between interdisciplinary interests and my own discipline. Studies in other areas help me understand my discipline better, but I always feel pressure to be doing more research in my own field."

What can be done to counter these forces which prevent more meaningful scholarly contributions by undergraduate faculty? Surely the answer is not more expensive journals. That is simply impossible.

But much could be done in less expensive ways to encourage faculty to continue the development of scholarly minds and to present their thoughts before critical audiences of peers. For example, a college itself or perhaps more fruitfully a consortium of colleges could sponsor inexpensive "journals" containing typewritten manuscripts. Submitted articles could be judged by an editorial board of peers and the publication could be circulated among interested colleagues in the college, the consortium or beyond. While the circulation would not be large, it would not be surprising if the actual reading of these articles would be more frequent than of some national journals.

Colleges could also do much more to encourage scholarly work of faculty simply by increasing the number of opportunities on campus for intellectual sharing and critical review. Faculty forums, public lectures, symposia and seminars are all useful and relatively inexpensive ways to encourage and recognize scholarly contributions of faculty. Several colleges, for example, have "faculty forums" in which faculty prepare and present papers to their colleagues on a regular basis. At St. Lawrence University where a forum in the humanities is held, one faculty participant remarked: "In this setting I have learned totally different ways of perceiving things. Our dialogue is worth nourishing." At Austin, St. Olaf, and a number of other colleges both students and faculty have benefited from the "last lecture" series. Under this format faculty present those ideas and values that they care most about—as if they were presenting their final lecture to the campus community.

At other campuses group projects or seminars have stimulated faculty to produce several individually or jointly written manuscripts for publication. A participant in a small interdisciplinary symposium at Trinity College, Hartford, remarked: "The symposium seemed to remove the burden of 'immediate production' which has forced me and many of my colleagues into narrow publication. The outcome for me was not only new intellectual stimulation but also several papers in my traditional area written with new perspective."

Most faculty publications focus on the subject matter in which they are experts, but faculty have much to offer others in another area in which they also hold expertise—namely, teaching itself. Faculty who are carrying out new approaches in teaching (or useful old ones) should be encouraged to put their ideas and practices on paper where other instructors could benefit. Several disciplines have journals devoted to pedagogical practices. Expanding this type of opportunity either within or across disciplines could encourage those faculty who perceive themselves to be primarily "teachers" to publish for the first time.

If any of these expanded outlets for new scholarship for faculty teaching at the undergraduate level are to have any meaning, recognition and reward must be given faculty who make contributions through them. They must be seen as legitimate means of scholarly exhibition. (Note: While much of the chapter has focused on publication, other means of demonstrating scholarly, professional work must be recognized. For example, artists, musicians, dancers must have good on-campus as well as regional or national opportunities for creative expression.)

To be sure these enlarged opportunities for scholarship will not carry the prestige of national journals or national artistic productions. Some of our faculty should and will continue to receive national recognition in various ways, but the large majority of faculty could benefit greatly from new scholarly opportunities, especially where (in the words of one faculty member) "renewal is the aim and not reputation." Hopefully, these enlarged opportunities will not only encourage all faculty to carry out more scholarly work but also allow those who already publish regularly to do so more meaningfully.

[1]Donald Light, *op. cit.*, p. 258.

Chapter 5

Renewing the Scholar as Teacher

On virtually all liberal arts college campuses the teacher-scholar is expected to be first and foremost a good teacher. Teaching usually ranks highest in criteria for evaluating faculty performance. The rhetoric of college catalogs, faculty handbooks, and recruitment statements usually points to the importance of good teaching. Therefore, liberal arts college faculty will surely welcome programs designed to enhance their teaching. Correct? No, dead wrong!

Obstacles for Teaching Improvement Programs

In examining efforts of faculty development on the campuses included in the AAC Project we discovered that programs aimed at teaching improvement were often among the least effective. Why was this so? At least three reasons come to mind.

First, there is a built-in attitudinal resistance to programs dealing with teaching improvement. This resistance is not hard to understand, for teaching is a deeply personal activity. As one faculty member emphasized: "Teaching is really tied up with who you are as a person. Changes in teaching behavior do not, therefore, come easily."

It was not surprising to hear comments such as the following during interviews with teacher-scholars: "I don't feel deficient in matters of teaching." "I think I already know how to lead discussions." "Programs in teaching methodology are Mickey Mouse. I'm satisfied with my teaching methods." These comments often reflect some important truths. Some teaching improvement programs are useless, and many faculty don't need to change their teaching habits, strategies, or styles. But others do need to be open to programs that can stimulate new approaches or revitalize old ones.

Attitudinal resistance is often revealed by faculty in less direct ways as well. For example, one faculty member at a college with an active instructional development program remarked: "It's too much trouble to get funds for special innovation." Another person argued that, "You need a gimmick to get the money." To be sure, some program directors are overzealous in calling for unique approaches, but in this case the faculty members may also have been saying, "Any deviation from my current teaching practice represents a gimmick."

Do these deep-seated attitudinal problems mean that teaching improvement is impossible? Hardly, for successfully operated programs and personal testimony belie the argument that important changes in teaching are impossible. But these attitudinal issues do mean that any program dealing with teaching must be carefully planned and sensitively administered.

A second reason for programmatic failures in teaching improvement is simply lack of both knowledge and imagination among program designers—and among faculty generally—in this particular area of faculty renewal. Interviews with individual faculty and with campus faculty development committees revealed how woefully unaware faculty were of the wide variety of approaches to teaching improvement being carried out on other campuses. A "Committee on Teaching Effectiveness" at one college spent three years floundering with the same ineffective approach before they finally began to investigate the experiences of other colleges. Another college committee, following two years of meetings, perceived that the *only* possibility for assisting their colleagues in teaching was having a "Master Teacher" from another college come and assist them.

To a certain extent it is important for a committee to come up with its own ideas and to speak to unique needs on a particular campus. Ideas from others cannot always be imported. But faculty—especially at colleges with a high degree of self-pride—often possess the false perception that they surely are at the forefront of thinking in whatever they are trying to do in faculty development. Can we really learn from some other "lesser" institution? Indeed, much time and effort could be saved and some exciting new thinking generated by examining some of the approaches of others, including the variety of possibilities for teaching improvement programs reported later in this chapter.

Built-in attitudinal resistance compounded with a lack of knowledge of program possibilities has led to a third reason for the low ratings of teaching enhancement programs, namely, poor program design. One common failure, for example, has been the tendency to overgeneralize. Several campuses have sponsored "Seminars on Teaching" or "Teaching Effectiveness Workshops," and most faculty participants have found these to lack good specific ideas useful in the classroom. On the other hand, where sessions dealt with specific topics such as "Considerations in Leading Discussion," "What To Do on the First Day of Class," "What Constitutes a Good Lecture," "Problems in Interdisciplinary Teaching," or "Using the Computer in Teaching Languages," faculty have felt they were able to carry with them from the session specific new skills or ideas. The impression was also given that these were sessions from which all teachers could gain, not just those who "needed improvement."

Another frequent problem has resulted from faculty "teaching improvement committees" falling into the "single-approach trap." On one campus a faculty committee was assigned the task of implementing the improvement of teaching aspects of a major externally supported faculty development program. The committee decided on video-taping faculty in classroom settings as their approach, spent a great deal of money on video equipment, and called for faculty to respond. Few did so. Though the committee later tried other approaches—discussions of teaching, visiting speakers, etc.—it always floundered under the image of being the "video-taping committee," and could not attract wide faculty support.

On another campus during an interview with a faculty member I asked: "Why does the faculty development program here not include anything dealing directly with teaching?" The reply: "Oh, I don't think that sitting in on a colleague's course is a good idea. The difficulty is that faculty won't be objective. They know too much!" Apart from misperceptions about the potential value of observing a colleague's class and giving feedback, this faculty member obviously had a very narrow view of teaching improvement possibilities. A single approach—sitting in—had been tried on that campus and no discussions were taking place that could encourage faculty to examine many other approaches.

What use should be made of a potentially helpful group of "experts" on the campus, namely, the education department? The *wrong* use of this group has led to another defect in program design. Some colleges have placed the entire program in charge of education department personnel; others have used them as authorities on the subject. This procedure has generally not been well received by faculty, who are suspicious of too much educational jargon and methodology. At one campus, one of the interviewers reported, "The idea of utilizing education faculty as teaching consultants failed miserably." More successful efforts occurred on campuses where faculty from other departments—chemistry, political science, history—were taking leadership in the teaching enhancement program, and education department personnel were used where needed as specialized contributors.

Setting the Climate for Teaching Improvement

Effective programs to assist good teaching can be designed and implemented. But they cannot be forced on a reluctant community. The stage must be set, a conducive climate generated. Campuses have been able to provide a supportive atmosphere in a variety of ways.

Special Committees and Projects. The establishment of a specific committee or implementation of a specific project is one way of saying that "teaching is important here," and "we believe that faculty should have opportunities to improve as teachers as well as scholars." For example, Colgate University set up a special council dealing with teaching-related projects. In the eyes of the outside evaluators, "the activities of the council at least raised the consciousness of faculty toward renewal focusing on instructional and curricular development. Previously funds for faculty development went only for research support."

In a special project, Earlham College faculty were interviewed systematically concerning their teaching. The major interview question was, "What have been the main influences on your development as a teacher?" (Those being interviewed were primarily senior faculty, the interviewers, primarily junior faculty.) As reported in the college's local teaching activities newsletter, the faculty interview project did not uncover "a previously hidden lever one can pull to improve the quality of teaching. It showed again how complex and individualistic teaching is. . . ." But it also demonstrated "the importance of good teaching. Perhaps most importantly, faculty were brought together in another way to talk about teaching, the chief function of an educational institution."[1]

Administrative Initiative. Ironically the promotion of an atmosphere which encourages good teaching must often be led by administrators. Because of the sensitive nature of teaching improvement programs, faculty themselves are not likely to initiate them. On the other hand, if administrators attempt to put together a program on their own, it will be viewed by faculty as being imposed from above and therefore strongly resisted. Result: a profound "Catch 22" situation.

One way out of this dilemma is for a key administrator—usually the academic dean—to enlist the aid of several key faculty members in program initiative, and as soon as possible to turn over leadership to a faculty group. This group can in turn solicit ideas and opinions from the faculty generally.

Faculty committees concerned with the enhancement of teaching must often be prepared to take initiative themselves in relation to their colleagues. For example, in the initial years of an outside grant the Colgate Faculty Development Council waited for activities to be generated by proposals solicited from faculty. Forthcoming were primarily requests for grants to individual faculty only indirectly related to teaching concerns. So the Council began to take leadership itself in organizing and finding activities designed to improve the campus climate for teaching.

Group Activities. As explained more fully in a later chapter, most of our faculty development activities have been individual in nature— sabbaticals, individual summer study projects, etc. Most faculty are not used to working *with* their colleagues on professional improvement. Thus, asking faculty to come together to deal with sensitive issues of classroom teaching requires for many faculty significant personal adjustments.

Some colleges have reported that the existence of scholarly or curricular oriented group activities by faculty may pave the way for subsequent activities focusing on teaching more directly. At Berea College, for example, faculty have for several years been engaged in seminars dealing with interdisciplinary curricular development. The college is now looking at potential programs aimed specifically at *teaching* improvement, and according to one outside observer, "It appears that the 'climate' for sharing ideas for approaches to teaching, if done correctly and sensitively, is improved as a result of all the sharing through the curricular seminars."

Openness to Experimentation. Among the various differences I noted in visits to the twenty liberal arts college campuses, one of the most easily discernable was to be found in the degree to which an institution was open to experimentation and innovation. On some campuses, new ideas were encouraged and taken seriously, on other campuses they were viewed automatically with suspicion.

At one campus an outside interviewer observed: "The faculty development program here has had very little impact on teaching except for new faculty. There is no climate for experimentation or examination of alternatives. Widespread acceptance of the traditional lecture course means few faculty want to look at their teaching in terms of 'new' ideas." Greater openness toward experimentation on a campus obviously facilitates discussion of both new and old approaches to good teaching. Such openness is not easily created on a tradition-bound campus. Beginning with a clearer understanding of the climate for (or against) experimentation on one's own campus is important in designing teaching improvement programs.

The Reward System. Where does teaching stand in the criteria for evaluation and reward? Are individual efforts to improve teaching acknowledged? At most liberal arts colleges teaching is listed first among the criteria for evaluating faculty performance. But the perception among faculty on many of the campuses we visited was that, despite what is stated in a faculty handbook, scholarly production or campus leadership activities were in reality more important in salary increases, reappointment, tenure, and promotion. Good teaching among a few "stars" on the campus was acknowledged, but the average faculty member seeking constantly to improve his or her classroom performance seemed to go unnoticed.

There are campuses where teaching is obviously highly valued, and faculty are rewarded primarily for their teaching performance. At Earlham College, for example, the president summarized what many faculty had earlier affirmed, "What we reward is classroom effort." There is, of course, a danger in an overemphasis on teaching, if it tends to discourage scholarly growth—which in turn can enhance one's teaching. That is not a healthy atmosphere for the renewal of the teacher-scholar. But to make no real effort to create an atmosphere in which good teaching is encouraged, expected, supported, and rewarded is equally counterproductive.

Effective Approaches to Teaching Development

Aided by a supportive climate, programs directed specially at teaching improvement can be designed and carried out successfully, despite the difficulties enumerated at the beginning of this chapter. Following are examples of such programs—examples which demonstrate that good teaching can be supported in a variety of ways.

Teaching Institutes. As pointed out earlier, teaching workshops or institutes which are too general in nature (like one labeled "Teaching Improvement Institute") are usually less successful. But workshops which provide opportunities for sharing specific ideas for teaching, consider both new and old approaches in particular teaching contexts, and arm participants with new skills, have been judged by faculty to be more beneficial.

For several years, under the leadership of Dr. John F. Noonan, Director of the Center for Improving Teaching Effectiveness at Virginia Commonwealth University, the Central Pennsylvania Consortium has provided an institute on college teaching for new faculty members at its four constituent colleges (Franklin and Marshall, Dickinson, Gettysburg, Wilson). While discussions on more general topics are a part of the institute, these normally arise from consideration of specific teaching situations. There is opportunity for "practice" where faculty teach something to their colleagues and receive critiques. There are sessions dealing with course planning, conducting discussions, enhancing lectures, etc.

Senior faculty at Franklin and Marshall, stimulated by the positive experiences of their junior colleagues, put together their own workshop. Most participants agreed with the opinion of one spokesman that "the most stimulating of the specific activities were the mini-lecture presentations to the group and the sharing of their reactions."

But designers of such workshops should never expect all faculty to profit equally from similar experiences. Faculty at the Franklin and Marshall workshop reacted as follows: "A very valuable experience." "Very worthwhile." "One of the most important events of my teaching career." But to the very same workshop, one faculty member responded: "A total waste of time." Just like students, faculty are not all alike, and it is important to structure programs in order to meet individual needs as much as possible.

Skill-oriented and Subject-oriented Workshops. Colleges have had very good experiences with skill-oriented seminars and workshops—for example, workshops on writing where faculty learn to teach and critique student essays as well as improve their own writing; or computer workshops where faculty learn how to utilize the computer in both instruction and research.

Faculty are often reluctant to give attention to methodology, especially if approached directly. However, some colleges have been able to give attention to pedagogical issues as a part of another focus—curriculum development, subject-oriented seminars, and the like. For example, at Austin College methodological concerns were considered as a part of seminars designed to prepare faculty to teach in the college's values-oriented Communications/Inquiry program. At Occidental College a workshop on non-Western studies brought fourteen faculty together to work on substantive aspects of a new integrated program. But also included were sessions on writing, leading discussions, and use of films in the classroom. At the same college an outside resource person helped faculty understand better psychological and physical barriers to language learning. At the same time the workshop included methodological "practice," focusing on specific techniques for classroom teaching. In each of these examples faculty were exposed to new ideas in teaching without having to face the decision—should I or should I not attend a workshop on methodology?—a situation in which many may automatically respond with a no, because they begin with an attitude that nothing worthwhile will be forthcoming or the topic may seem too threatening.

The Senior Colleague as Mentor. There is a tradition in higher education that senior faculty serve as mentors to junior colleagues, encouraging them in their scholarship, giving them feedback about their teaching, introducing them to campus politics, i.e., assisting their development as teacher-scholars. But this tradition seems to be observed less and less in the academy in recent years. Junior colleagues are often left on their own to fight for limited tenure slots. Senior faculty are reluctant to assist faculty who may be around only a few short years; or in encouraging their younger colleagues, they may seem to be giving false hopes toward those they must later judge in relation to tenure. Junior faculty perceive their senior colleagues as setting up stiffer criteria for tenure than the established faculty themselves can meet. The result is tension between the two groups, and the mentor-student relationship is virtually impossible.

Still, some colleges are trying to counter these trends. Senior faculty on some campuses are recognizing that they have a professional responsibility to assist new faculty, no matter whether they will be at their institution for three years or thirty.

Furman University is one such institution trying to renew the mentor tradition. Under a formal program faculty with established teaching skills share their experience with junior (and other senior) faculty in both regularly scheduled group workshops and in one-to-one sessions. In the workshops senior faculty have dealt with topics such as the following: "Ways of Individualizing Instruction," "Asking Questions," "Uses of Media," "Testing," "Development of Reasoning: An Application of Piaget to College Teaching," "Non-Verbal Communication," "The Role of Affective Processes in Learning," "Examining Learning Theories," "Making Outlines for Lectures," "Teaching from the Imagination: Self-Images of the Teacher," "Lecturing: The Teacher as Actor," "Leading Discussions." In individual sessions, senior faculty will visit their junior colleagues' classes and give feedback, or invite them to observe their own classroom teaching.

In evaluating the Furman program, one outsider observed: "For those faculty involved in these activities, manifest concern for teaching is something they now share in common, making continuing conversation easier." The program, in his view, has allowed faculty to "analyze their teaching needs and produce new insights by articulating areas in need of development and designing projects to meet the needs." Faculty have developed "new areas or expertise for presenting content to students and familiarized themselves with new (at least new to them) teaching methodologies." Participation in the program is often a real confidence-builder for younger faculty as they observe experienced colleagues. As one young Furman teacher remarked: "I discovered that faculty who had been here ten to fifteen years had the same problems as I."

But serving as a mentor is not a one-way "welfare exercise." Senior faculty recognize that they profit as well—for they are forced to re-examine their own philosophies and practices of teaching, and they gain helpful insights from both senior and junior colleagues in the program. Levinson in his book, *Seasons of a Man's Life,* stresses the need for a person at some point in life to have a mentor. It may be that mentorship is also equally important to the one who consciously is called upon to serve in such a role.

Taking a Colleague's Course. At Haverford College several pairs of faculty have agreed to take a course from each other in the hopes of then fashioning an interdisciplinary, team-taught course. For example, a political scientist and an English teacher combined to create a course in political thought and literary expression in pre-Civil War America.

But the experience of taking a colleague's course went far beyond learning something of another's discipline. New ideas and understandings in teaching were gained as well. One Haverford teacher observed: "I learned a lot about teaching while being a student in my colleague's class. For example, I never had realized how effectively the blackboard could be used in facilitating and summarizing discussion." Having a colleague in the classroom added some extra incentive for careful preparation. Admitted one faculty member, "The presence of my colleague made me work a lot harder!"

For many faculty the idea of having a colleague sit in their classrooms, especially throughout an entire semester, is very threatening. The classroom is often viewed as the teacher's private kingdom to be entered only by the students. But for those faculty who have been able to open themselves and their classes to their colleagues, the experience has usually been richly rewarding.

The Teaching Consultant. To whom do faculty members go when they want some assistance concerning their teaching? Many fear that they will be revealing "weaknesses" if they go to their department chairperson or dean. Faculty are often reluctant to give honest feedback to their colleagues. The result is often a frustrating feeling of isolation for many faculty.

Earlham College has attempted to counter this problem through a faculty member who serves half-time as a teaching consultant to other faculty. Although the consultant is appointed by the dean, the appointment is based on a comprehensive polling of faculty to determine whom they would most trust in this role. The consultant carries out his activities in strict confidentiality—visiting colleagues' classes at their request, counseling teachers concerning student evaluations of their work, helping in course planning, giving advice to faculty experimenting with new courses or new approaches to teaching, and being helpful in a variety of other ways as needed. In order to separate the consultant from the formal evaluation process, he or she may not serve on any faculty personnel committee for at least three years after his consultancy is completed. Surprisingly, during the four years of this program more than seventy per cent of the Earlham faculty have sought assistance from the teaching consultant.

The role of the teaching consultant is an extremely sensitive one, and the two faculty members who have been consultants thus far, Jerry Bakker of the chemistry department and Paul Lacey of the English department, have recognized this. Bakker emphasized that the consultant must "work with the teacher and be responsible to him, not to the students or administration." He must not see himself as "an expert on teaching methods, not an educationist, not a pusher of a particular methodology," but instead "take the person seriously in relation to his own discipline." Above all, the consultant must be seen as continually supportive. Lacey exemplified this positive approach when he stressed that the consultant must assist the faculty member in putting "all his strengths in the right places." Faculty members should call to mind assistance received from the consultant "in what they're doing when they are at their best." The college, in its report to the Fund for the Improvement of Postsecondary Education, recognized the same point: "Teaching is such a personal matter and the ego-involvement of teachers is so high, that any consultant who is more critical than supportive is likely to lose his audience and thus any chance to be effective."

How have faculty reacted to the teaching consultant at Earlham? In the on-campus interviews faculty testified—as a result of either personal experience, or observations of others' experiences—that changes in competence, self-confidence, and specific skills have occurred. They were also appreciative of having someone to go to—to receive help with small, yet important, teaching problems. As the college's report to FIPSE observed: "It was surprising to discover how many teachers found autonomous control of their courses to be a lonely position. Many need simply to talk about minor course matters, something which is inhibited by concern about 'professional dignity' among colleagues. Yet minor matters can be important in how a student perceives a course and one's learning." One faculty member summarized the benefits of the teaching consultant when he said: "It has reduced a lot of tension about teaching."

Lawrence University has also made use of the teaching consultant idea, although less extensively. In this case a retired, well-respected professor of theater is available to sit in classes and gives "private lessons" to faculty focusing on their classroom presentations, including voice placement, diction, and style. The retired faculty member provides a valuable, non-threatening source of support when needed.

While the teaching consultant program involves primarily one-to-one relationships, the long-term impact may significantly affect the teaching atmosphere of the entire campus. Claude Mathis in his evaluation of the Earlham College program states his belief that "over time, the college will begin to develop a core of faculty who are trained to analyze and recognize effective teaching in the many disciplines. . . ." In his view, faculty who have utilized the consultant "should become more identified with the mission of Earlham College and with the need to be continually monitoring their teaching activities. Both the consultant and the client become part of a larger support system which not only establishes expectations about excellence in teaching, but also provides specific procedures for making this excellence operational."[2]

Other Programs. The potential variety of approaches to assisting teaching on liberal arts college campuses is almost endless. Some colleges have established *awards for outstanding teaching* as an incentive. In certain instances the award has produced more ill feeling than good teaching—as a result of jealousy, suspicious selection procedures, etc. However, on two of the campuses in the AAC survey, teaching awards received generally positive reactions. Students, administrators, and faculty saw them as a good way to say "Teaching is of great importance here," and careful selection procedures led other faculty to affirm that "Those people deserved the award."

St. Olaf College six years ago established its *Teaching/Learning Center,* a physical and programmatic center which brings faculty together to share ideas on teaching and related issues. Led by a team of faculty associates, the center sponsors mealtime discussions, special workshops and provides a seminar-reading lounge housing material on student development, improvement of teaching and other important areas of higher education. Increasingly faculty have been willing to not only come to discussions and seminars, but also to initiate and take leadership in the TLC sessions.

Dickinson College has for several years sponsored a *classroom observer program* which provides faculty members with a trained student observer for a semester. The student, while not a registered member of the class, observes and evaluates the teacher and meets with him or her regularly to give feedback. Non-participants often look with a skeptical eye on the program, but most faculty who have worked with an observer has appreciated the student input and many have altered courses and approaches to teaching (or felt more confident about continuing the same approaches) as a result.

Many other approaches to the improvement of teaching could be listed and described. The above descriptions provide a representative sampling that may spark further experimentation and program development. Each campus must assess its own needs and take into account how and when faculty are likely to respond most positively.

The story is told of a conversation between a farmer and the local extension agent. In response to being given by the agent a pamphlet on farming methods, the farmer replied, "I think I already know how to farm twice as good as I'm able."

Some faculty will take the same attitude toward improvement of teaching programs: "I already know how to teach twice as good as I'm able." And, indeed, that statement may be true for a few faculty. But most can and will profit greatly from programs designed to reassess old and stimulate new ideas about teaching.

The teacher-scholar usually understands quite readily the importance of keeping up in the discipline and of pursuing scholarly work. A few scholars are indeed "natural teachers" and don't require active participation in the programs described in the chapter. But most faculty, in order to be true *teacher*-scholars, must recognize that growth and renewal as a teacher are needed and are possible throughout an academic career.

---

[1]Teaching and Learning Committee, *A Learned Journal*, (Richmond, Indiana: Earlham College), Volume 2, No. 1, October 15, 1976.
[2]Claude Mathis, Evaluation Report, Earlham College, 1977.

Chapter 6

The Need to Focus on Students

Understanding Student Development

Surprisingly, indeed alarmingly, a very basic element in the educational process is usually overlooked when colleges are designing teaching improvement programs, namely, the *students*. In recent years researchers in higher education have increased significantly our understanding of student development. Works by Astin, Katz, Heath, Perry, Sanford, and others have helped us appreciate that students, even those with quite similar academic backgrounds, come to college with differing perspectives of the world, with differing interests and attitudes about the most interesting and effective ways to learn, differing moral and ethical reasoning, differing stages of development. These researchers have emphasized that what really makes an impact on students in the long run is not the exact content of a course, but the outlook, the perception, the sense of appreciation that students bring with them from a course and from college generally.

But do faculty have these issues in mind when designing and teaching improvement programs? Usually not. One college visited in the AAC Project had a major grant to revise its curriculum. But all efforts centered on course content and none on the students. In designing faculty development programs colleges very infrequently looked at their student clientele, and the possibility of significant change in that clientele in the 1980s.

This lack of attention to student needs and differences is disturbing, yet understandable. Faculty are "trained" in graduate school to focus almost exclusively on their disciplines. They are socialized rapidly to think of themselves as historians, chemists, political scientists, etc. rather than educators in a broader sense. Thus, most faculty are simply not attuned to focusing on students when exploring questions of learning and teaching and most are quite unaware of the rich variety of higher education literature dealing with student development.

Fortunately some colleges are becoming aware of this serious omission as they work to revitalize their academic programs and their faculty. At Berea College, for example, there were clear signs of faculty awareness of *student* perspectives. Program leaders in the college's major interdisciplinary core courses have urged faculty participants to concentrate on student learning needs and differences. A teacher in one of the core courses agreed with the emphasis: "In teaching an interdisciplinary core course there is often too much concentration on getting the faculty ready to teach. We must also focus on the question, 'What are students learning?'"

At Furman University many of the seminars in their Lilly-supported faculty development program have centered on student development and the learning process. One faculty member admitted that at the college "there is a lot of disagreement about whether we are here to teach students or to teach a course." But in contrast to most campuses, there was at least open discussion about student learning problems and potential. During my visit to the campus I witnessed a seminar in which a member of the music faculty was sharing his ideas on learning theory with colleagues from several departments. His concern was that too many faculty operate by what he calls the "hope theory" of learning, that is, "I present the material and hope they learn." In his presentation he demonstrated an awareness of major theories of learning and showed how his classroom style and organization conformed with specific theories. Another Furman faculty member revealed her understanding of these same issues in an article written for the faculty newsletter, where she stressed: "Students have different learning styles, that is, they don't all learn the same thing in the same way at the same time." This has important ramifications for teaching: "One difference in a skillful teacher and an unskillful one lies in what each perceives about his students as individual learners."[1]

At Gettysburg College a new committee on "the teaching-learning environment" emerged from a faculty seminar on student development. Led by psychologist Douglas Heath of Haverford, the seminar stimulated new thinking about student intellectual, social and moral growth and differing approaches to meeting student learning needs. The committee, which includes faculty, students, and administrators, is an ad hoc group aiming to establish a more permanent monitoring committee on "the learning environment" of the campus.

Some teacher-scholars have a kind of natural sensitivity toward student problems and differences. But most can profit from workshops, seminars, or readings concerning new understandings of student development. When faculty are more sensitive to the variety of stages of intellectual and moral growth among students, they are likely to examine more carefully the content of their courses. When faculty recognize that students can and do learn in a variety of ways, they are likely to explore alternative, sometimes more effective modes of teaching.

Focusing on student development is also a valuable way to get at improvement of teaching for another very important reason. It is less threatening. The same faculty who are often reluctant to come to a session on the improvement of teaching where the focus is directly on them may be quite willing to attend a workshop or seminar where the focus is on the students—but in the long run have their own teaching affected, perhaps significantly, by new perspectiveness on student learning and development.

The Teacher-Scholar as Adviser

One of the often neglected roles of the teacher-scholar is advising—serving as an informed and sensitive counselor to students in their academic program and its relationship to career and other personal decisions. Good-and-poor advising can have a major effect on a student's life. Yet, in my travels for the AAC Project it was discouraging to discover that very few colleges in their faculty development programs were giving any attention to this important non-classroom aspect of being a good teacher.

Out of the twenty colleges visited, only one, Colgate University, had systematically given attention to improving faculty advisers. As one of the outside interviewers stated, "This is one of the few examples where a grant provided any support for the advising role of the faculty." A workshop was held, a faculty advising handbook produced, and another workshop for freshman advisers is being planned.

When faculty think of their own development the focus is usually only on their classroom teaching and their scholarship. Very rarely in the AAC interviews would a faculty member speak of his or her need to improve in advising or other non-classroom roles. One exception was a faculty member at Austin College who in his "Career Development Plan" had set forth a specific program for improving himself as an adviser, including being evaluated by his advisees.

Studies have shown that good advising can have an impact on student retention. In these days when enrollment problems are acute it seems wise for colleges to give some attention to developing faculty as advisers. But even if such problems were not before us, care and concern for the development of students should lead us to improving our advising programs—and our advisers.

---

[1]Hazel Harris, "Beliefs about Education," . . . *And Gladly Teach*, Furman University, Sept. 1978, No. 1, p. 5.

Chapter 7

Renewing the Content of Teaching

Woodrow Wilson, during his presidency of Princeton University, is alleged to have said, "Reforming a college curriculum is as difficult as moving a graveyard." Most administrators and faculty would agree that there is a great deal of truth in Wilson's statement. Why is curriculum change so difficult? It is not because the curriculum in and of itself resists change, but because those who teach and administer the curriculum need their perspectives broadened from time to time. As John Gardner emphasizes, "Men who have lost their adaptiveness naturally resist change. The most stubborn protector of his own interest is the man who has lost the capacity for self-renewal."[1]

Curriculum Renewal and Faculty Renewal

Thus, curriculum renewal and faculty renewal must go hand in hand. Curricular change cannot be carried out without faculty adapting themselves to new course content and approaches to teaching—unless curriculum change is defined as simply reshuffling the same old courses or giving them fancy new titles.

On the other hand, curriculum renewal can be a great stimulus for faculty renewal. Changing individual courses, reforming majors and academic programs, and forging new interdisciplinary approaches often force faculty into valuable renewing experiences required for program implementation.

Changing curriculum is, of course, primarily for the benefit of the students, but the *process* of change and preparation may have greater meaning for the faculty. One of the leaders in Kenyon College's newly formed Integrated Program in Humane Studies observed: "This new program is of great value to the students, but perhaps more so for the faculty. The faculty learn new areas and gain new ideas in teaching."

A new curriculum cannot be implemented without giving faculty time and resources to make the necessary changes in their courses, to learn new material, to develop new perspectives. At Berea College a new core curriculum was adopted by faculty in the early 1970s, but initially support for implementation was lacking and the new program faltered. With the obtaining of outside funds, faculty were then given the opportunity to work together in summer seminars to prepare for teaching four interdisciplinary core courses: "Issues and Values," " Religious and Historical Perspectives," "Man and the Arts," and "Christian Faith in the Modern

World." Funds were also provided for faculty needing individual study time to prepare for teaching in areas outside their regular fields. In the eyes of Bill Stolte, Berea's academic dean, "The curriculum would have fallen apart, if it had not been for the faculty development opportunities provided by the Mellon grant."

Faculty renewal in relation to curriculum must be a continuing dynamic process. There are some faculty who can teach the same course throughout their academic careers, use virtually the same materials and techniques, and still provide a top-notch course. But most faculty simply cannot operate that way. Courses need to be changed, not simply because the content needs to be updated, but also because the teachers need recharging. This is also why some colleges make a concerted effort to rotate faculty in and out of courses and programs. At Austin College, for example, which in the early 1970s undertook several major curricular reforms, one faculty member who had been with the same inter-disciplinary team for several years surmised: "The real problem is tired blood. It is hard to generate enthusiasm at staff meetings. We have heard the same ideas too often from our colleagues." Austin is a college which has a sensitivity to continuing faculty renewal in relation to its cur-riculum, and will look to not only rotation of faculty but also broader curricular adaptions in order to keep a strong academic program.

Curricular change has another important relationship to faculty development. It is a generally "acceptable" focus of renewal. Many fac-ulty will not get involved in a program labeled 'faculty development" but may get involved in quite similar experiences if they are labeled "cur-riculum development." Just as focusing on students is often an effective, yet less threatening, way to get faculty to reconsider their teaching so can focusing on curriculum be an effective, less threatening means of engag-ing faculty in renewal of both teaching and scholarship.

Even among the more active scholars on campus curriculum reform can play an important role. As earlier chapters have emphasized, schol-ars at liberal arts colleges can often be led to concerns that are narrow or questionably relevent. As one faculty member at Bowdoin stressed, "Having funds aimed at specific curriculum reforms can provide an im-portant challenge to the more active researchers to pursue areas helpful not only to them but to the broader liberal arts goals of the college."

Liberal arts colleges are currently using a variety of approaches that link curriculum renewal and faculty renewal. Hope College, for example, has held month-long workshops during the past several summers to pre-pare faculty for teaching in the Senior Seminar, the "capstone" course of the Hope curriculum which merges questions of faith and learning. The workshops have made use of both local resources and outside "experts" to help faculty understand new perspectives of faith and ethics in relation to their own disciplines. Faculty at Bowdoin have received small grants to develop new, experimental courses for the curriculum or to make ma-jor changes in existing offerings. In my visit to Bowdoin, several of their faculty indicated that these new curricular offerings would not have been possible without the challenge of these "faculty development" grants. Denison University has provided similar course development grants for its faculty; St. Olaf College and Bates College have aimed their challenge grants at departments, calling upon departments to act collectively in revising majors and fashioning new curricula. Many approaches are possible, but in planning for such programs it is important to recognize where faculty renewal and curriculum change must go hand in hand.

A Word of Caution: Curriculum vs. People

In liberal arts colleges today the curriculum must be built around people—that is, around the existing expertise and interests of the faculty. It will not be possible for most colleges to dream up a radically new curriculum and have the financial resources to bring in new faculty with new expertise to staff the program.

Nor should we try to push existing faculty into narrow, predetermined slots. Several times we encountered faculty members who had enthusiastic interest in a particular subject area but were prevented from teaching in the area by a department whose consuming goal was to "cover" some ideal curriculum. Which is better, to allow the curriculum to dictate what each faculty member should teach, or to allow for some flexibility, providing an opportunity for a professor to teach a particular course with special excitement and interest? At one college, sensitive to these issues, a senior faculty member observed, "You must make it possible for a person to show his strengths and enthusiasm in his area."

One college visited in the AAC Project had adopted a program of leave grants, designed to encourage faculty to explore new areas within their disciplines or in related fields. However, very few responded. Why? Several faculty admittted in interviews that the psychological and intellectual adjustments of moving from their "regular" fields were simply too overwhelming, but most saw the inflexibility of the curriculum as the culprit. "I would very much like to learn about and teach a course in film literature, but my department won't allow it." "Although I am in the English Department I have a great interest in teaching a course that would benefit the history program, but that department will not permit it." "There appears to be no reward, from the department or college, for studying in the area of my real interest."

Of course there are legitimate limits to curriculum flexibility in a liberal arts setting, but a program should be shaped at least in part in response to people and not always people in response to program! The discipline or department is a time-honored way of organizing knowledge. Its value has been proven. But this does not mean it should be the dictator, the final determinant. It should enhance learning and teaching, not stifle it. It should not prevent new adventures in faculty renewal that can make both faculty and students excited about learning and teaching.

The Interdisciplinary Challenge

The small liberal arts college is viewed by many outsiders as the place where the integration of knowledge takes place naturally and frequently. Unfortunately, such is often not the case. Meaningful interdisciplinary programs have been and are being created on liberal arts college campuses, but the task is not easy, and the obstacles are often greater than anticipated.

To begin with, graduate schools do not prepare faculty to think in interdisciplinary terms. In fact, many faculty are trained intensively in "sub-disciplines" and struggle to learn to teach more comprehensive courses in their own disciplines in the initial years of their academic careers.

Still, many younger faculty take appointments at liberal arts colleges with the expectation that interdisciplinary opportunities lie ahead—only to be disappointed when they don't appear. Why is this the case?

During an interview at one of the liberal arts colleges visited in the AAC Project, one faculty member remarked: "Interdisciplinary study should be left to the student in a place like this. Why should a faculty member have to pursue interdisciplinary work. It is better to have disciplinary experts in a few fields." Most faculty would not state their opinions so directly but many support such a view, for at most colleges, interdisciplinary learning *is* left to the student.

Faculty who do desire to venture into interdisciplinary learning and teaching often do not receive support from their department chairpersons. The department head views such interdisciplinary excursions as taking something away from the department's program. (And in fact he may be right—in the sense of a department "losing" a particular course, or teaching it on an every-other-year basis. But of course the same "excursion" could also be seen by a less defensive department chairperson as the faculty member "representing" the discipline's point of view in a broader context, thereby extending the department's program, not detracting from it.) Faculty are also cut off from teaching in interdisciplinary areas by other departments who are "suspicious" or feel threatened. For example, I recall vividly interviewing an English department member who had a great desire (and the proper credentials) to create and teach a course linking English literature and history, but was blocked from doing so by that college's history department.

Faculty need professional support, and usually that support comes most readily from their departmental colleagues. Wider support and recognition come from national discipline-oriented professional organizations. Recently, Adele Simmons accurately described this natural orientation as follows: "Among academics little prestige is earned by teaching students who major in other fields, much less by teaming up with colleagues from alien departments, or by engaging in other peculiar activities suggested from time to time by advocates of interdisciplinary learning."[2]

All these reasons placed together constitute an immense amount of pressure on faculty to stay within their discipline. It is simply unrealistic to expect faculty under ordinary circumstances to create new inter-disciplinary programs or respond quickly to existing opportunities. Here again is where faculty development and curriculum development mingle. Faculty, with administrative leadership and support, must be challenged to accept opportunities to reach beyond their disciplines, explore new perspectives, and learn from colleagues in other departments.

A number of colleges visited in the AAC Project have undertaken suc-cessful interdisciplinary-oriented faculty renewal programs. Bringing faculty together in seminars to learn from each other has been both popular and effective. Trinity, Berea, Kenyon, Occidental, and many others have used this approach. The seminars have not only helped faculty learn new material but also have been responsible for many other important benefits for individuals and the colleges, as enumerated in the later chapter on "Faculty Renewal: Individuals vs. Groups." Haverford College encouraged two faculty members to take a course from each other with the goal of eventually merging the two courses. For example, a political scientist and English teacher interrelated their disciplines for a course on "Goethe and Beethoven." This is a relatively inexpensive way of developing a new interdisciplinary course. Also, the courses were given double-credit, thereby allowing faculty to get full credit for teaching the course and reducing departmental fear of "losing" a course.

Faculty who have participated in such interdisciplinary experiences have found that they have been able to overcome some important per-sonal, psychological, and intellectual barriers. A Berea faculty member remarked: "When I started interdisciplinary work, the most important problem was a psychological one. I was trained to emphasize my discipline and get rewarded there. The real problem was getting over the 'terror' of dealing with new material, admitting I didn't know something and would not be the 'great expert' teaching the students." Another Berea faculty member in economics had a special leave to study in philosophy and theology at Vanderbilt, in order to prepare to teach the inter-disciplinary "Religious and Historical Perspectives" course. "Before I went to Vanderbilt I could not have done more than spell Hesiod, let alone teach something about him," he admitted, but the leave gave him "confidence to attempt the course" and his enthusiasm for such a teaching opportunity is great. Another faculty member who had been through an interdisciplinary seminar spoke with appreciation of "the ability to look at the world through another window."

But these kinds of interdisciplinary experiences on a campus will be short-lived unless additional basic structural changes take place. There must exist an on-going mechanism for establishing interdisciplinary courses—where "room" is provided in the curriculum to test out such courses. At one college development grants were provided to encourage faculty to do research and study in other fields, but great frustration resulted when faculty discovered that no provisions had been made for teaching courses related to their new learning.

Some colleges have instituted "interdisciplinary departments" which have been allotted a certain number of faculty slots or FTE's. Called by various names, "University Studies," "College Courses," etc., these programs provide room for experimentation. Headed by a director who has status equivalent to a department chairperson, these arrangements also provide an important built-in advocate for interdisciplinary work on the campus. This person can also ensure that faculty teaching in interdisciplinary courses are given proper recognition by the dean and others. In the final analysis, if interdisciplinary teaching is to succeed, faculty must perceive that they will be rewarded and supported by key administrators for their efforts. Especially since rewards for such faculty are not likely to be forthcoming from national professional organizations, deans and presidents must make sure that on-campus recognition is meaningful and visible.

The disciplines should and likely will always be the major way to organize teaching and learning. But at liberal arts colleges we must make manifest our rhetoric about the importance of the integration of knowledge. We must demonstrate to ourselves and our students that knowledge—and certainly wisdom—cannot always be compartmentalized, that problems often demand comprehensive solutions, and that we really do care about "the whole person." A faculty member at Hope College, who had been an active teacher in the college's interdisciplinary capstone Senior Seminar, described to me how his participation had given him "a firmer sense of what it meant to be at Hope" and a "better understanding of the college's whole curriculum." And then he made this compelling statement: "The liberal arts ideal at a church-related school is often a shimmering mirage, but the Senior Seminar has made it incarnate." Liberal arts colleges—in both curriculum and faculty development— must continue to accept the interdisciplinary challenge.

---

[1]Gardner, *Self-Renewal*, p. 10.
[2]Adele Simmons, "Harvard Flunks a Test," *Harpers*, 258 (March, 1979), p. 26.

Chapter 8

Improving the Environment for Renewal

More than anything else continuing renewal of the teacher-scholar requires an environment which encourages such renewal. John Gardner has pointed out that persons who are self-renewing testify almost universally that "certain kinds of environments smother their creative impulses and other kinds permit the release of these impulses. The society interested in continuous renewal will strive to be a hospitable environment for the release of creativity."[1]

In the AAC Project on Faculty Development one of the issues to which we gave careful attention was the extent to which a college had reorganized itself to create an ongoing favorable environment for renewal. Very few had done so. Out of the twenty colleges surveyed only six had instituted some organizational or structural changes designed to enhance faculty renewal, and these changes were in most cases relatively minor in scope and impact.

It is of course extremely helpful for a college to put more money into faculty development, to obtain outside grants, to institute some of the programs in teaching improvement, scholarship assistance, and curricular change described in earlier chapters, but these programs must be undergirded by more fundamental changes. In the long run specific changes in structure and practices of the college itself may have more impact than any other approach to faculty development. It is ironic that college faculty and administrators will often study and provide consultation concerning the importance of renewal in other kinds of organizations, but neglect the environment surrounding themselves. John Gardner also notices this irony in academe: "The same incomplete approach to innovation may be seen in our universities. Much innovation goes on at any first-rate university—but it is almost never conscious innovation in the structure or practice of the university itself. University people love to innovate away from home."[2]

Faculty may not be giving systematic study to organizational changes required in liberal arts colleges to encourage renewal, but they are quick to point out deficiencies which affect them personally. During the interviews in the AAC Project, comments were frequently made by faculty in five specific areas, where changes in college policies and practices could make a significant difference in faculty attitudes toward renewal. The five areas: the reward structure, the committee system, on-campus faculty support systems, personnel management, and faculty evaluation policies (covered separately in the next chapter because of its great importance).

The Reward Structure. Many faculty we interviewed described their campus reward systems as very unclear. Would personal efforts at renewal really be rewarded through salary increases or promotion, or at least acknowledged in some form or other on campus? To what extent will new scholarly production or sincere efforts at improvement of teaching be rewarded—or even noticed on campus? Faculty do pay attention to signals given by colleagues on review committees, department chairpersons and deans concerning expectations for teaching and scholarly production. But often faculty remarked during an interview, "I don't know what the criteria are. The policies keep changing." Where signals and expectations are unclear, the positive impact on renewal is often lost.

In a few cases the reward policies were clear—but discouraging. The impression was left with faculty that *only* scholarly production, or more rarely, good teaching, would lead to significant salary raises or promotion in rank. This tilting of the balance scale may be necessary for emphasis from time to time but in the long run this one-sidedness is not helpful to the development of the teacher-scholar.

The Committee System. Structural changes in the faculty committee system need to be given attention in two specific ways in relation to faculty development. First, committee involvement of faculty members is often excessive and even sometimes irrelevant and unproductive. Committee systems tend to grow as new issues arise on campus, new rules are introduced to the faculty handbook, and old committees keep operating—whether they are needed or not. Teacher-scholars must take responsibility in key areas of governance—especially in overseeing curriculum and academic standards and assisting with personnel evaluation—but from time to time a college must examine whether committee responsibilities for faculty are too heavy. One college, following a series of faculty summer seminars in which teacher-scholars learned to know and trust each other better, reduced the number of committees from approximately eighteen to six. In interviews on that campus several faculty commented on the positive impact of the new system on their teaching and professional development.

Second, in whatever committee system is operative, faculty development must have a prominent place. It must not be assigned to a minor sub-committee. Interviews with faculty indicated that having a group of respected teacher-scholars (working with key administrators), overseeing faculty renewal from a prominent place in the committee system, was an important factor in a successful faculty development program.

Unfortunately, several campuses in the AAC survey had given no thought to where faculty renewal issues would be handled in the committee structure. This meant that issues, needs, and programs were never discussed systematically on campus. At one college, I asked: "Is there a place or process for discussing faculty development needs for the future?" The honest answer was, "There is none." In reference to that same college the other outside interviewer wrote: "The grant has not wrought any fundamental change, nor could it, given the lack of a local mechanism to assess goals and design faculty development activities to help meet these goals."

St. Lawrence University is a good example of one campus which understood the need to give faculty development a prominent place in the governance structure. After receiving a grant for faculty development, the college created "The Academic Resources Board." Composed of nine faculty appointed by the President and chaired by a well-respected retired physics professor, the Board took responsibility for soliciting faculty ideas, defining faculty renewal needs, and implementing programs. Following a series of experiments using small grants, and additional feedback from faculty and administrators, the Board produced a "Systematic Plan for Faculty Renewal," setting forth both short-term and long-term goals for faculty renewal at St. Lawrence.

Another important reason for giving faculty renewal a prominent place in the governance structure is that faculty development and institutional development must be carefully interrelated. Furman University recognized this crucial issue in its 1977 proposal to the Andrew W. Mellon Foundation: "It is probably no longer possible or desirable to view faculty development as a wholly individualistic enterprise unrelated or only tangentially related to institutional goals. While faculty members' personal goals cannot be ignored, in a time of crisis in higher education, it is important for them to understand the ways in which their individual development is inextricably bound up in the welfare of the institution." If faculty development issues are handled by a key committee on campus, they can be more closely related to the larger institutional goals. If such issues are handled by a committee operating at the periphery—or not dealt with systematically at all—the development of the college's most crucial resource, namely, the faculty, will be lost among competing goals.

On-Campus Faculty Support Systems. I recall vividly one interview with a faculty member in which I asked him what the most important faculty development needs were on his campus. His answer: "Additional secretarial help." His point was well taken. He had attended, and gained from the sessions on his campus dealing with teaching improvement. He was working on an important scholarly manuscript. His major need at the moment was secretarial help to complete the manuscript, along with help for regular departmental correspondence he was forced to type himself.

Faculty development is not always a matter of teaching workshops, intellectual seminars, individual study grants, or curriculum adjustments. Colleges need to provide—to the extent that budgetary considerations will allow—a variety of basic on-campus support systems. Adequate secretarial help is one example. Some colleges have a small fund to assist faculty in obtaining and paying for additional secretarial help, if the campus secretaries cannot take on typing a major manuscript. Another area frequently mentioned by faculty was having a person on campus designated to help individuals obtain grants from foundations and government agencies. This can be a person in the development office or in the dean's office. In the case of St. Olaf College, the Coordinator of Academic Grants reports jointly to the Vice President for Development and Planning and the Academic Dean, and has provided valuable assistance to faculty in obtaining outside grants.

Providing good library and media services is also for many faculty a key component in faculty development. On several campuses I visited, library and media center directors were themselves becoming more aggressive in demonstrating to faculty how they could better utilize their services. Providing proper equipment, especially for science faculty, is often another important element in faculty renewal. Liberal arts colleges cannot afford the major pieces of equipment housed at large universities, but an active research (and teaching) program can be carried out by faculty at undergraduate liberal arts colleges, if certain kinds of equipment are purchased and maintained.

Travel to professional meetings has become extremely expensive. One also wonders how valuable some professional meetings really are. But the answer for faculty renewal is not to do away with a travel budget altogether. It is important that faculty are able to get to a professional meeting at least every two or three years. Many colleges are also providing special support to faculty who are presenting papers at professional meetings, as an incentive for scholarly development and contributions.

Personnel Management: The Crucial Role of Department Chairpersons. Interviews throughout the AAC Project unfortunately reaffirmed that "personnel management" continues to be an area of weakness in our colleges. Frequently faculty members complained of not receiving feedback concerning evaluations, not knowing what changes in salary recommendations meant for them, not getting personal encouragement for their research or teaching. It is, of course, the responsibility of presidents and deans to see that these personnel issues are dealt with. But they themselves cannot ordinarily reach every individual faculty member personally, unless the college is very small. Thus, the key person in personnel matters—including faculty development—is the department chairperson.

The most important responsibility of a department chairperson ought to be the recruitment, evaluation, development, and continuing renewal of faculty within the department. Yet, other responsibilities seem always to gain more prominence—class schedules, ordering equipment, monitoring the budget, and so on. Moments are rarely found for sitting down with a faculty colleague, providing feedback on evaluation, asking about research projects and new ideas in teaching, encouraging applications for professional development, or passing along a supportive observation from a colleague.

That department chairpersons often give less attention to such sensitive personnel matters is not surprising. Department chairpersons usually enter their role with little or no training in evaluation procedures, counseling, and faculty development. Some learn these new duties quickly, others remain extremely uncomfortable in attempting to handle these issues. The problem is exacerbated by the trend toward more rapid rotation of department chairs, often every three years, which has caused many to think of the chairmanship position as simply a temporary "caretaker" role.

Throughout the visits to the twenty colleges in the AAC Project faculty and administrators testified to the need to give more attention to the role of department chairpersons in faculty development. Several deans characterized the current role of department heads in relation to faculty renewal on their campuses as "minimal." At one college with a relatively good program of faculty evaluation one of the outside interviewers commented, "However, evaluation does not seem to have such impact. Most department heads do not provide any feedback to the faculty being evaluated." At another institution department chairpersons were clearly depending on an associate dean to counsel their faculty members concerning evaluation and development. He in turn reluctantly characterized department heads as a "weak link" in the faculty development program of the college. Another young, untenured faculty member at the same college summarized the lack of interchange with department heads in this way: "All younger faculty must go through a three-year review. If you have problems, you get called into the dean's office. Otherwise you hear nothing." At another institution severe personnel problems developed when several persons were denied tenure, not simply because the decision was negative, but primarily because the decision came as a total surprise to the faculty involved, for they had received no earlier counsel or warnings from department, division heads or the dean.

This lack of communication on personnel matters not only creates animosity and confusion concerning evaluations but also prevents some faculty from being more active in personal growth and renewal. Personal encouragement and rewards of praise or at least acknowledgement of interest are important to people—including faculty. Also, some faculty will simply not respond to general announcements and memos concerning faculty development opportunities, no matter how often they are sent, but personal signs of genuine interest can sometimes make the difference.

Not all comments received from faculty during the AAC Project interviews were so negative concerning the department chairperson's role. Some comments revealed very careful and sensitive personnel practices of department heads. At Bowdoin College a young faculty member commented: "During my first year here my department chairman took time to observe my class six or seven times. I was in his class three or four times. He was very helpful to me in my teaching." At Hope College one of the outside interviewers wrote in his report: "One of the divisional deans obtained a professional development grant at least partly so that he could model the type of behavior he wanted to see his faculty adopt. Numerous comments were made to me how chairmen had encouraged their faculty to submit or resubmit their grant proposals (to the college's professional development committee)." Similar positive reports were heard concerning the work of specific chairpersons at various colleges.

Unfortunately these strongly positive comments concerning the role of the department heads in faculty development were the exception rather than the rule. Yet, it is a serious mistake to blame individual department chairpersons for this situation. In the long run it is the *college's* responsibility to help department heads understand and prepare for this important part of their work. I interviewed a department chairperson at one college who recognized the low level of personnel skills among department heads on the campus, himself included, but he emphasized, "No one has been telling me how to do it better. We have had no meetings for department chairmen as a group in years. There seems to be a lack of center in the college. We need a sense of direction in these matters."

Some colleges have recognized that department chairpersons, instead of being a "weak link" in faculty development, can be a strong force for renewal on the campus. For example, one of the interviewers following a visit to Furman University wrote: "More than at any other college thus far, there was discussion of the important role of department chairmen in the faculty development process. Also, several faculty remarked that there was encouragement by department heads for involvement in the various programs." The college was attempting to obtain an outside grant for training department chairpersons in personnel management. Trinity College in Connecticut has also devoted some of its outside grant monies to developing department heads in similar ways.

As academics we have traditionally not been very sensitive to the great importance of personnel matters on our campuses. Our "subject," our curriculum, almost always is at the center of our attention. Yet, in recent years we have been forced to deal with personnel considerations by the larger society in response to economic and salary problems, affirmative action, and decreasing opportunities for faculty mobility. Our response to these concerns, however, has usually been a *legalistic* one, writing into our faculty handbooks rules and regulations for all kinds of situations, yet never being quite able to anticipate and handle them all. There could have been another response—perhaps there still can be. We can and must give more attention to developing better "people managers" in the best sense of that phrase, people (department chairpersons, deans, presidents, colleagues) who understand the importance of giving honest yet sensitive feedback, support, and encouragement, people who in the long run will be trusted at least as much as the legalistic paragraphs of the faculty handbooks.

John Gardner has written: "We must discover how to design organizations and technological systems in such a way that individual talents are used to the maximum and human satisfaction and dignity preserved."

And he emphasizes, "The whole purpose of such knowledge is to design environments conducive to individual fulfillment."[3] Liberal arts colleges must continually ask, are we providing environments conducive to individual renewal and fulfillment? Asking that question will cause us hopefully to not only envision new ad hoc programs, but also re-examine our reward structures, committee systems, faculty on-campus support mechanisms, personnel management practices, evaluation systems, and other aspects of our organizational environment. In doing so we may very well touch some of the most important, long-lasting ingredients in renewing our teacher-scholars.

[1]Gardner, *Self-Renewal*, p. 35.
[2]*Ibid*, p. 76.
[3]*Ibid*, pp. 64, 65.

Chapter 9

Faculty Evaluation and Faculty Development

On virtually every campus visited in the AAC Project we frequently heard faculty—and administrators—voicing serious complaints about the evaluation system. Most faculty understood the importance of having a good, comprehensive evaluation system, most said they would welcome evaluative feedback on their work, but most said they simply did not trust the current evaluation system on their campuses. In their eyes the system was filled with too much bias, not comprehensive enough, not reflective of their work, not specific enough in relation to possible areas for improvement.

Without doubt these criticisms sometimes stemmed from a posture of defensiveness and self-indulgence. But the criticisms were widespread enough to indicate a more critical problem, a problem which has serious ramifications for faculty renewal. A good, well-respected evaluation system can be extremely helpful in faculty development, the absence of such a system quite detrimental. It is needed not only for providing a fair assessment of faculty performance for "administrative" purposes but also for indicating strengths and weaknesses. A reasonably accurate, non-threatening evaluation system can be an important stimulant in faculty renewal.

Problems in Faculty Evaluation. What were the concerns voiced most frequently by faculty concerning evaluation? Criticism focused not only on the system's design but also on the way it was administered and on its underlying assumptions.

Just as there is frequent confusion as to what the college expects of its faculty as teachers and scholars, so is there confusion about evaluating faculty performance. At one college, one of the outside interviewers reported: "There is great concern and confusion on the campus about evaluation. Each department is to develop its own system. Non-tenured faculty especially are looking for more precise criteria. Is teaching still number one? Is research gaining ground? Is service to college and community really unimportant? The major faculty committee unfortunately has deliberately stayed away from the topic of evaluation." A good evaluation system is not possible without clearer expectations as to what is important in faculty performance.

Evaluation was also frequently viewed as uneven and unsystematic. At another campus an interviewer observed: "The college has a variety of evaluation methods. There is a three-year review required for non-tenured persons, but nothing for tenured faculty. There is the perception that evaluation is not very systematic and varies too much among departments." On that campus the faculty development committee was making specific plans to re-examine the evaluation system, because they understood its implications for their own goals in faculty renewal.

Evaluation was frequently viewed as a threat because it was almost always "summative"—for purposes of salary review, reappointment or non-reappointment, tenure review, etc.—and only rarely "formative"—for purposes of self-improvement. Many faculty hope to teach in an environment which encourages self-development and the development of others, where one competes more with oneself than with others. Instead they find themselves in a situation where they seem to be constantly competing, and comparative evaluations for summative purposes encourage such competition. Claude Mathis, asked by Earlham College to examine the college's faculty evaluation system, outlined his belief that: ". . . student evaluations of teaching should provide evidence of directions for further development rather than evidence of comparisons of the extent of development at a fixed point in time in relation to colleagues. Much of the anxiety I sensed in my interviews may result from the discontinuity which younger faculty feel when their non-competitive expectations are suddenly confronted by an evaluation system which suggests competitive comparisons." Mathis reports that this anxiety is especially acute for younger faculty: "Some see student evaluations as a 'stress test' and a 'puberty rite' whose function is to 'separate and weed out' rather than help and improve." Robert Lisensky, also asked by Earlham to comment on the college's evaluation system, voiced a similar concern for all faculty: "Even the 'best' of the faculty find it hard to be constantly judged in relation to others."[1]

Heavy reliance on quantitative systems has intensified the competitive atmosphere on our campuses. Quantitative approaches, by their very nature, require comparative analyses. Mathis, in the same report mentioned above, maintains: "Most faculty members seek higher education as a non-competitive environment for self-expression. Quantitative evaluation, particularly of teachers by students, leads to competitive expectations and a change in the nature of academic environments." Lisensky, writing independently warns: "The battle with numbers leads to a sanctification of the tool itself (class evaluation)."[2] As a result of these criticisms, an Earlham faculty committee concluded that the evaluation process was "too rigid, formal and impersonal," and the college has made a number of important changes. Ironically, Earlham, in comparison with other institutions, already had a very supportive collegiate atmosphere; the need for changes in evaluation systems was much more pronounced at most of the other colleges visited in the AAC Project.

In some cases faculty themselves have been responsible for unsatisfying, often haphazard, approaches to evaluation by their refusal to deal seriously with the issues. Some faculty would like to avoid any system of evaluation. But evaluation cannot and will not simply go away. Even on campuses that have no formal system evaluation does take place. Colleagues talk informally—often without accurate information—about their colleagues. Students drop by the offices of department chairpersons or deans to comment on specific teachers. These forms of evaluation are, of course, very unsystematic and usually detrimental rather than helpful to faculty. So the question is not, Should we have an evaluation system? It is rather, How can we create a comprehensive, fairer, more highly respected system?

Where faculty have refused to deal with the issue, students have often moved into the breech. Most of the time this has resulted in the publication of selected student comments on specific courses or the creation of a quantitative, comparative system. While there is some value in both of these approaches, they have not ordinarily been helpful to faculty renewal. Faculty and administrators must not ignore the challenge to design and implement for themselves an evaluation system that will provide not only relatively accurate information for summative purposes but also encouragement for ongoing personal development.

Evaluation and Development. Another problem encountered at many of the colleges in the AAC Project was that even where a systemic evaluation program was in place faculty did not receive helpful and sensitive feedback from the evaluators. This, of course, prevented the key linkage between evaluation and renewal from taking place. Time and again we asked faculty, "Who on this campus meets with you to provide evaluative feedback and give advice on development opportunities? At one campus, an associate dean was credited with counseling faculty and giving encouragement to pursue specific new activities in their externally funded faculty development program. One outside interviewer commented: "Even this link, although weak, is more than one finds on most campuses." Davidson College demonstrated an understanding of the important relationship between evaluation and development, when in their recent "Code of Evaluation Procedures" they stated: "Davidson's faculty evaluation procedures must be closely related to institutional strategies for faculty development. Students are quick to perceive which of their instructors are active professionals, which are merely living on past capital. Good teaching requires continual study to keep up with developments in one's field and to achieve that understanding of related fields so important to the idea of liberal education. The evaluation process and opportunities for development must be linked in such a fashion as to nurture and encourage profession growth."[3]

A good faculty development program requires a good faculty evaluation system—and vice versa. Without good faculty development opportunities evaluation for purposes of renewal is hollow. A faculty member, who goes through an evaluation process, receives specific suggestions, and honestly desires to strengthen himself or herself can rightly ask, "Will the institution provide assistance for improvement?" An active faculty development program provides a positive answer to the question. Faculty evaluation and faculty development must be closely related for the benefit of both.

Positive Approaches to Evaluation. Is it possible to create a comprehensive program of evaluation in which faculty will have a relatively high degree of trust? According to interviews in the AAC Project, the answer is yes, as long as the program follows four important guidelines: 1) the utilization of a variety of sources of data, 2) the existence of opportunities for both summative and formative evaluation, 3) heavy involvement by the faculty in designing the system, and 4) the extension of the system to *all* faculty in the college.

1) Faculty feel especially threatened—and with some justification—when only one source of data is used in evaluation. This is especially true when the single source is comparative student evaluations. Fortunately such systems have become more sophisticated, flexible, and helpful in recent years; some colleges were, for example, making good use of nationally tested systems such as the Kansas State IDEA program or the Purdue CAFETERIA system. But even these programs are limited in perspective. Many other forms can provide potentially very beneficial data for both the individual faculty member and the college: student essay evaluations, classroom visitation by colleagues, letters from alumni, interviews, videotapes, peer comments on scholarly work and public presentations, and self evaluation.

Self-evaluation is often downgraded because of its obvious potential bias, but in the AAC Project we witnessed its effective use in several cases. For example, at Austin College each faculty member must provide a plan for his or her own evaluation as a part of the career development plan. The evaluation scheme must specify by whom the evaluation is to be conducted and by which methods. For example, one faculty member in his career-development plan focusing on the next four years detailed the following persons and methods: "From departmental colleagues, open-ended written evaluations; from students, standard statistical forms and some oral interviews; from division chairmen, open-ended written evaluations." Observation and evaluation by other persons are solicited, but the responsibility is on the faculty member to present a comprehensive evaluation package concerning his performance as both teacher and scholar. In the eyes of most faculty, having the freedom to choose from several forms of evaluation also allows more room for experimentation; a single approach often discourages faculty from departing from well-worn paths to which students have become accustomed.

Can the self-biases in such self-evaluation processes be eliminated? Probably not entirely, but administrators and department chairpersons can recognize quickly when a faculty member is skewing the results by selecting only certain persons or methods for evaluative feedback. Colleges should look more seriously at providing and encouraging the use of a variety of sources of evaluative data, and allowing faculty some freedom in choosing those methods most appropriate to their own disciplines, teaching, and scholarly goals.

2) Presidents, deans, department chairpersons, and faculty personnel committees need good sources of data to make reasoned, fair judgments

of faculty for promotion, tenure, salary increments, reappointment or non-reappointment. A summative, "administrative" evaluation system must exist with a variety of sources to carry out this function well. But there must also be opportunity for evaluation outside this formal system, primarily for formative, self-development purposes. Otherwise evaluation tends to be viewed by faculty members as primarily an attempt to discover weaknesses.

Of course, summative and formative evaluation cannot and should not always be neatly separated. Administrators ought to encourage further development on the basis of recommendations they receive. Faculty ought to feel free to submit voluntarily evidence gained during formative evaluation processes to deans or department chairpersons for use in making personnel decisions. The major concern, however, must be to create an atmosphere in which faculty see evaluation primarily as a helpful tool in faculty development—as worthy of their time and energy and as an encouragement to renewal and growth.

3) Faculty will not put their trust in a system in which they have not played a major role in designing and implementing. An effective evaluation system will be recognized as "their own" system. It cannot be imposed upon them. We visited campuses where an evaluation system had been initiated either by administrators or by students. To be sure the system was providing some useful information for personnel decisions, but it had virtually no standing in relation to faculty growth and renewal. Administrators will often have to *lead* faculty (by suggesting, cajoling, convincing, enlisting the support of faculty leaders) into designing good, comprehensive evaluation systems, but in the long run it should have the faculty's own imprimatur.

4) Finally, to be successful an evaluation program must include *all* the faculty. On many of the campuses we visited formal evaluation systems included only the non-tenured faculty. This was damaging in two ways. It caused resentment among non-tenured faculty and provided no help for tenured faculty seeking to renew themselves.

Several colleges, however, were seeking to alter this unevenness and require periodic evaluation for both non-tenured and tenured faculty. For example, Earlham College in addition to its regular assessment of non-tenured faculty, adopted a review requirement for tenured faculty on a five-year rotation. Under this system a committee of three faculty members works with the tenured faculty member during the year of assessment, assisting with the evaluation plan, providing feedback, and finally submitting to the dean a report which is shared also with the faculty member. The dossier ordinarily contains self-evaluation statements, student evaluation forms, letters from present and former students, letters from faculty colleagues both inside and outside the department and additional relevant documentation. The emphasis at Earlham has been to use the five year review for personal growth. Remarked one faculty member who had been on a review panel: "The first two meetings with the committee are sometimes fraught with anxiety, but 'shape up or ship out' is definitely not the posture. We want our faculty colleague to grow in the ways for which he is best suited." According to Earlham President Wallin, the review has for some faculty meant a rededication to teaching, and a concentration on "how good the future can be, not how bad was the past." He also believes the review process has improved the quality of proposals for sabbatical leaves and the college's professional development fund. However, in a few cases, as a result of the review process or other counseling, faculty members have decided to move out of the teaching profession, or are considering it seriously. (A similar instance occurred at Austin College when a faculty member selected another career as a result of his struggle to write his long-term professional growth plan.) The question can be asked: Should the institution in such cases provide faculty development funds to assist the person to move into a new career? In these instances, the college, out of concern for the individuals, answered the question positively—and I believe, rightly so. But for most Earlham faculty the five-year review led not to a drastic shift in their careers, but to reaffirmation of teaching. Still, in the words of one faculty member, "It was an important time for reality testing."

Faculty development can benefit immensely from faculty evaluation— especially where the evaluation system provides a variety of data sources, concentrates on assessment for formative reasons, has strong faculty backing, and touches both non-tenured and tenured faculty. In such systems, the level of trust appears to be higher and the results greater.

---

[1]Claude Mathis and Robert Lisensky, "Reports on the Evaluation System at Earlham," July, 1976.
[2]*Ibid.*
[3]Davidson College, "Code of Evaluation Procedures," draft version, December 1, 1978.

PART III

The Process Of Renewal:
Key Issues

Chapter 10

The Importance of "How"

To this point we have concentrated on *what* colleges have been attempting to do to renew the teacher-scholar. In this section we turn to the equally important issue of *how* programs in faculty renewal have been or should be carried out. Throughout the AAC Project on Faculty Development we gave attention to not only the *content* of faculty development programs but also the *process* of designing, implementing, and managing such programs.

During an interview on one of the twenty campuses, an administrator observed correctly that: "Innovations are not accepted on their merits." Indeed we were struck by the fact that quite similar programs had quite different impact on different campuses. Thus, *how* a college goes about planning and carrying out its renewal program is equally as important as *what* it proposes to do—in certain instances perhaps more important.

Several process-oriented issues emerged as especially important during the on-campus interviews. This chapter will give attention to the key elements of purpose, planning, and communication, along with brief attention to program management and program evaluation. Because of the importance of the issue, there follows a separate chapter on the question of individual renewal vs. corporate renewal.

Purpose

Why are we concerned with faculty renewal? What specifically are the needs we must address on our campus? Many colleges had failed to ask and seek to answer such questions in designing their faculty renewal programs. As a result objectives were often unstated or stated in such broad terms as to be almost meaningless. One college proposed in a planning document to "examine future needs and make necessary adjustments." Another said that the purpose of its renewal program was "to get faculty out of regular routines via a variety of approaches," but then failed to specify which routines and which approaches.

Another institution seemed to be more specific in its goal "to increase effectiveness in liberal education by enhancing curricular flexibility and by encouraging versatility in our faculty." Yet, during interviews there seemed to be confusion among both faculty and administrators as to how much emphasis was to be given to "curricular flexibility." What impact on the curriculum was expected from the renewal program? To what extent was interdisciplinary work being encouraged? Lack of clarity on such questions left faculty confused as to what was expected of them and whether renewal efforts would be appreciated.

Colleges sometimes also failed to examine their *needs* carefully before launching a faculty development program. If a college decides beforehand that its real need is improving the scholarly climate of the campus, the program's purpose will be much different than a college where curricular or classroom teaching needs are deemed of greater importance. But if a college fails to sort out its needs and program purposes, the result is usually lost time and poor placement of precious resources.

Planning

Careful planning—or lack of it—can have a significant impact on the success of a faculty development program. Most colleges in the AAC study recognized this fact, but in several instances planning was too brief and involved only a small handful of individuals.

I recall the motto of a community organization in the inner-city of Philadelphia: "Plan or be planned for." Most people do not like to be "planned for." The same is true with faculty. At one or two of the campuses we visited it appeared to be acceptable for planning to be carried out by a few administrators. But at most colleges failure to involve a significant number of faculty in the planning process can—and did—lead to problems. At one campus, planning had been carried out largely by administrators, several of whom by the time of our campus visits had departed for positions in other colleges. Faculty support on that campus for the current faculty development program was not very strong, as one might readily suspect. In another instance a college was hurried into preparing a proposal for funding in faculty development by the funding agency's midsummer deadline. The college, using a small committee, quickly put together a proposal—a relatively good one—but the program, when funded, had a hard time getting off the ground; faculty interest and response were slow in coming and not very enthusiastic, for they perceived it to be "someone else's" program.

Faculty and administrators often have differing perceptions as to what is most important in faculty development. These differences can be resolved, but only if enough spadework has been done, so that their differing perceptions are clearly understood. At one campus the original goals for a faculty renewal program involved primarily moving faculty into several new curricular areas. But these goals were seen by the faculty as primarily "administrative" and became much less significant when the program was essentially placed in the hands of a faculty committee. The committee took a year to redefine the program, gain both faculty and administrative support, create more positive attitudes, and then launched a much stronger program for the benefit of both individual faculty and the college's larger goals. The point seems clear: Meaningful faculty involvement in the planning stages of a program calling for *their* response is crucial. Such involvement creates a feeling of faculty "ownership" of and long-term commitment to the program.

In recent years many colleges, in response to projected enrollment problems, inflation, energy concerns, and other issues, have undertaken special efforts at long-range planning. Yet, faculty development often seems to be ignored in such efforts. One college, for example, established a planning task force in preparation for a ten-year accreditation visit. They worked hard at deciding long-range goals and objectives, but, as one of the interviewers reported, "Surprisingly, faculty development was not a part of this long-range planning." The current chairman of the college's academic planning committee admitted that "this is a task we should probably take up."

It is extremely difficult to make specific long-range plans for a college—or any institution. Many have tried to plan in some detail for ten-year periods only to learn later that major adaptations are necessary. Still, a college can make sure that its institution will have a "built-in" mechanism for renewal. Including faculty development in such planning is one means of providing such a mechanism. Faculty renewal must be a part of institutional planning, if a college intends to keep itself alive and lively.

Communication

At relatively small liberal arts colleges one would think that communication would take place fairly automatically. Faculty would know what their colleagues were doing in both teaching and research. News about faculty renewal opportunities would spread through informal gatherings on the campus. Such is not the case, however, even in small colleges. Formal communication networks must be established, for we found through our interviews that where such networks were missing, the faculty development program was affected negatively.

At most colleges there was adequate information concerning the *opportunities* for faculty renewal. (However, I recall that in one interview when I mentioned a relatively major program of grants available for faculty, the interviewee replied, "Oh, do we have such a program?") The biggest communication problem was lack of information concerning program *results*. Faculty on several campuses were largely unaware of the renewal efforts of their colleagues in both scholarship and teaching. At one campus, an interviewer reported, "On-campus communication has been extremely poor. Faculty remember the first announcement, but few had any ideas about who and what faculty development funds were currently supporting. There is a real need for communication and sharing."

Similar assessments of communication problems were made by interviewers at other colleges. One reported, "Communication seems to have been good with regard to the college receiving the outside grant and its availability to faculty. But in terms of the uses to which the grant has been put, there is a blatant absence of recognition among faculty (other than those who were directly involved)." Another interviewer in relation to a different campus wrote, "All of those with whom I talked were familiar with the *opportunities* and apparently this was true in general throughout the faculty. However, the *results* of the program do not appear to be well-known across the campus. Faculty know that there is a program of small grants, for example, but are unclear to whom they were awarded or what the outcomes were."

Communication of program activities and results can be carried out effectively in several ways. Some excellent examples were found on the campuses we visited. Furman University, for example, puts out a regular bulletin entitled, "And Gladly Teach." Earlham has a similar publication. St. Olaf has its "TL Courier," a publication of the Teaching Learning Center. Each of these publications describes professional development programs and activities on campus, reports on previous events, often summarizes individual scholarly work or new approaches to teaching, and indicates new books or other materials related to teaching which might be helpful to faculty.

Key academic administrators must carry out their responsibilities for good communication. At Hope College, for example, the provost not only announces new faculty renewal opportunities but periodically summarizes previous awards. In the eyes of one outside interviewer, the provost had done "an excellent job of keeping faculty well informed of both faculty development opportunities and of projects funded." Interviewers were convinced that these practices had a positive impact on the renewal program.

Another approach to good communication is the on-campus forum. At Mt. Holyoke, for example, all recipients of faculty development grants are required to make a public presentation upon returning to the campus. Other colleges have established regular "Faculty Forums" where faculty can share with colleagues, students, and others their scholarly work and interests.

Why is good communication so important in carrying out an effective faculty development program? For one thing it is a crucial ingredient in building a supportive scholarly community. A social scientist at one campus remarked, "The dearth of communication around here about the professional aspects of what we are doing has led faculty, especially younger ones, to feel isolated." Communication and sharing of scholarly ideas can help overcome the isolation which often arises from departmental structures and age divisions among faculty.

Most importantly good communication concerning faculty development activities can serve as a helpful stimulus for more faculty to consider their own professional development needs and to take advantage of opportunities for renewal. On campuses where both opportunities for development and results of programs and projects were reported frequently interviewers found that faculty often responded, "If he can do that, so can I," or at least, "That sounds worthwhile exploring." Where communication was inadequate this potential "bandwagon" effect disappeared.

Program Management and Evaluation

Interviewers in the AAC Project were not surprised to learn that program management made a significant difference in faculty development. What was important in management? In one word, *leadership.* Who was leading made an immense difference. Administrators had to learn when to assume the leadership mantle and when to step aside in favor of strong faculty initiative and influence. Which faculty were given leadership roles was an important issue. If the program were turned over to a subcommittee chaired by a junior faculty member, program impact was severely weakened. If faculty who were respected by their colleagues and thoroughly supportive of the program were enlisted for leadership roles, the chances for a successful program were greatly increased.

Another key element in the management of any program is periodic evaluation. This is especially true in dealing with the sensitive area of faculty development. Interviewers were disappointed to learn that systematic evaluation of faculty development efforts was not being carried out very frequently on the campuses visited. Too often the response to interviewers' queries in this area was, "We are thinking of doing some evaluation at the end of the faculty development grant period." Lack of careful evaluation after one or two years of experimentation meant that several unproductive programs were unwisely carried forward, without modification.

Evaluation must be considered a regular part of the faculty renewal program. Dean Whitla of Harvard University has made five very useful suggestions for incorporating evaluation into the development program: 1) Assign someone the task of evaluating at the *beginning* of the program. 2) Put together a pre-program and post-program evaluation design, and in the process explore and profit from what others are doing. 3) Combine several different evaluation methods (quantitative, qualitative, surveys, interviews, etc.). No one approach is best. 4) Always strive for objectivity. 5) Stress the *use* of your evaluation results. People are more likely to cooperate in the evaluation process if they recognize that their opinion might be helpful in revising and improving the program.

Because faculty development is such a troublesome, sensitive, yet crucial area in which to try new (and old) approaches, colleges that build systematic, periodic evaluation into their renewal programs will reap major benefits.

Chapter 11

Faculty Renewal: Individuals vs. Groups

Individual Renewal. We must never forget that in all our efforts at faculty renewal we are trying to affect the lives of individuals. This is no easy task, for individuals differ widely in their inherent capabilities and in their resistance to or openness to change and growth. As the recent informative works of Daniel Levinson, Gail Sheehy and other writers on adult development have emphasized, what may work for one person at a particular stage of life may not work for another person at a different stage.

It is not surprising, therefore, that most of our programs of faculty renewal have been individual in nature. This is clearly the case with our most traditional faculty development programs—sabbatical and special leaves, travel to research libraries and professional meetings, nationally competitive grants for summer study or year-long research and writing. These types of activities usually mean that faculty are doing research on their own in a library or a field situation or traveling to a conference where they may interact with faculty from other colleges, but usually not from *their own* institution.

This type of development in which faculty receive salary, travel, and other financial support to pursue primarily their own purposes has usually been accepted quite easily by faculty, especially by the active participants. (Sometimes those on the sidelines may look with suspicion on the kinds of activities for which their colleagues receive local or outside grant funds.)

These programs of individual opportunities for faculty will always be needed. Most persons in academe will quickly be able to think of several faculty who have returned from an individual study leave with a sense of accomplishment and a renewed vitality for teaching and continuing scholarly activities on campus. Persons need opportunities to pursue their own strongest interests, and not only they but others around them usually can benefit from their doing so. Individual activities, moreover, can provide more flexible responses to meet the different needs of both individual faculty and individual disciplines.

As the earlier chapters on professional development indicated, colleges have been providing some very useful new approaches to individual renewal. Institutions have altered budgets to put more money into competitive grant programs for individual research, travel, and study. Even relatively small grants, if carefully allocated and administered, have proven to be a great stimulus to many faculty. Other individually oriented programs such as faculty exchanges with other colleges, internships for faculty in nonacademic settings, and individual counseling programs for teaching assessment and improvement, have been found helpful and meaningful. Some colleges have also attempted to provide new support for traditional programs. For example, recognizing the real financial problems for faculty trying to take full-year sabbaticals on half-pay in the face of burdensome inflation, several colleges have been increasing their sabbatical support grants out of their own budgets.

These individual opportunities for faculty renewal must be kept alive. But a college for a variety of reasons (many of which are just now coming into clearer focus) should not put all of its faculty development resources into individual activities.

The Need for Corporate Activity. Currently there are so many forces that tend to sunder and insulate faculty members. The graduate school years orient people so well toward their professions (defined in disciplinary terms) that reorientation toward broader questions and perspectives of other disciplines is a very difficult task. One faculty spoke sadly in observing, "We seem to have gone so deeply into our professions. We need to share and talk." At another campus a faculty member, thinking of the pull of the disciplines, pointed out that, "Our intellectual networks lead off campus. We have lots of isolated individuals here."

Growth in enrollment and faculty size on many campuses in the 1960s and early 1970s brought new forces that tended to divide faculty. Increase in the size of faculty usually meant additional, often more particularized, courses. In thinking of this situation one faculty member remarked that he was often left with the following feeling toward faculty in other departments: "I don't really know who you are or what you are teaching." Growth also encouraged small but significant physical changes—faculty offices were spread out over the campus, usually arranged by department; the "community coffee pot" was replaced by the departmental coffee pot. Some faculty also perceived a decrease in community events on campus which had previously provided time for sharing and communicating.

Throughout our visits to the twenty campuses it was not uncommon to hear faculty describe lamentably their local situation as follows: "The faculty is split." "Individualism is rampant here." "We have focused so much on our individual and departmental needs. Now we need to think about the question: What does it mean to be a faculty?"

Ironically colleges have unwittingly encouraged this "isolation" and false "professionalization" of the faculty through their own programs of faculty renewal. By supporting sabbaticals, travel to professional meetings or other types of individual research and study as the *only* means of faculty development they have worked counter to their own stated goals of integration of knowledge, community and colleagueship. At one campus the chairman of the college's faculty development committee unknowingly but quite explicitly revealed this irony. Just after stressing the work of his committee in assisting a variety of individual professional development projects and the necessity for doing more of the same, he observed: "We need to develop more camaraderie among ourselves, to encourage each other more." At that same campus one of the interviewer-consultants wrote in his report: "It may be that the individual nature of most of these projects could have reinforced the 'natural' tendency of college faculties toward isolation and fragmentation."

Examples of Faculty Renewal via Group Activities. Fortunately some colleges have begun to react quite deliberately against these isolationist tendencies of faculty. They have brought faculty together in seminars, workshops and other group settings to share intellectual perspectives in some very helpful and stimulating ways. A few examples:

Kenyon College, out of concern for faculty compartmentalization, ran a series of summer seminars for four summers. With approximately twenty-five in each seminar, eventually about eighty percent of the faculty participated during the four-year span. During the initial two years the seminars focused on Kenyon's philosophy of education, but in the final two years the focus shifted from "talking about the liberal arts" to "doing the liberal arts"—tackling broad substantive issues in an interdisciplinary manner.

At Occidental College the faculty seminar format was different. Seminars were held during evenings over a three month (or sometimes longer) period during the academic year. From five to fifteen faculty discussed a topic with the aid of a visiting scholar. Subjects included: structuralization, values, policy analysis, energy, South Africa, feminism, and information theory. In thinking about the current seminars (which are aided by outside funds), one Occidental faculty member remarked: "Seventeen years ago a group of faculty used to do this on their own. Then came the late 1960s and the drive toward specialization and professionalism."

The above two examples were not involved directly with curricular considerations. Hope College provides a good example of a successful group activity tied to curriculum improvement. The Hope summer workshops brought together faculty involved in the Hope Senior Seminar, the college's "capstone" course which seeks to integrate questions of faith and learning. Four to five weeks in length, these workshops assisted faculty in preparing to handle questions of faith and ethics in relation to their own disciplines. Both on-campus and outside resource persons were used.

Several other valuable group approaches were observed. At Davidson College, an informal faculty research group meets once per month in which intellectual sharing follows the reading of a prepared paper. At Trinity College small interdisciplinary symposia were held during the past several years (five to six faculty in each). Focusing on subjects such as "language and observation," "nineteenth century perceptions of the individual" and "explanatory forms and models," faculty worked together during a period of several weeks in the summer and continued discussions during the academic year. At Colgate a special seminar on the liberal arts is providing an opportunity for several faculty and a group of students to discuss and debate matters of scholarly, intellectual interest.

Benefits of Group Experience. How did faculty react to these types of corporate activites? While some disappointments were reported, faculty almost universally found real benefits from these experiences—often in some surprising ways.

New intellectual perspectives were often gained by serious intellectual interaction with faculty, especially those from other disciplines. Looking back on seminars and workshops with their colleagues, faculty reported: "The seminar increased my respect for the way in which persons from different disciplines attack a problem." "I realized that in our group at the deepest level we are all doing the same thing. Intellectual, imaginative processes are much the same." "It made me more skeptical of some of the things I am doing in my own disciplines." "It was very worthwhile to learn what questions are important to colleagues in other fields."

An unexpected outcome for both planners and participants was the new appreciation and respect for their colleagues which faculty gained. Comments by faculty ranged from a simple growth in familiarity, ("We got to know each other very well." "I feel I will know X as long as we both teach here." "I have a much better perception of my peers.") to more profound alterations of perspectives, ("He was much brighter and articulate than I had ever given him credit for." "I gained a sense of warm personal regard for other faculty." "We were finally beginning to build each other up and demonstrate respect and interest." "We began to break down false perceptions and stereotypes.").

Perhaps most importantly these group intellectual experiences gave participants a sense of being a corporate body—a faculty. They helped to break down departmental isolation and identification. Faculty began to think of themselves as "a community of scholars working at the same basic goals." One faculty member expressed a similar thought as follows: "The seminar gave me the opportunity to believe that I was part of an academic team." Following an institute on teaching for senior faculty at one college, an evaluation committee report expressed the "faculty-building" aspects of the experience as follows: "Among those who participated in this institute, there was a strong and widely shared impression that its real value lay in the development of a shared sense of purpose, of colleagueship, of a mutual exchange of ideas and support that rarely occurs in our day-to-day interactions on the campus."

Other important benefits of group activities were reported. Administrators and faculty at one college were convinced that faculty meetings improved as a result of a series of seminars. There appeared to be less "one-up-man-ship" in the meetings and more open, honest, and thoughtful debate. Other colleges reported that many faculty who might normally not step forward to take advantage of faculty renewal opportunities were "pulled into" these group experiences by noting the interest of their colleagues. Also, the group approach to faculty development is often quite cost effective. A significant number of faculty can be included for a relatively low cost.

Faculty we interviewed who had taken part in seminars or institutes at the national or regional level (for example, the NEH Summer Seminars) were generally very enthusiastic about this type of learning experience (depending, of course, on the quality of leadership). Several remarked that since so much of the learning experience for students is corporate, why shouldn't faculty pursue and enjoy learning in this way more often as well—and why shouldn't they do so on their own campuses.

Individual opportunities for scholarly development and study will continue to be crucial, but colleges would do well to put a goodly amount of their faculty development funds also into group experiences.

PART IV

Final Challenges

Chapter 12

The Challenge of Administrative
Leadership and Support

To be successful a faculty development program must have strong administrative support. But support means more than tacit approval. The kind of support necessary is that which is reflected in the comment of one college president: "Faculty development is so important that it should not be seen as a fringe benefit."

Administrative support must be reflected in financial commitments. I was impressed with the budgeting allocations made by several liberal arts colleges to ongoing faculty development, following the expiration of outside grants. In one case a college with less than one thousand students had set aside from its own budget more than $60,000 per year for faculty renewal activities, above and beyond the regular programs of sabbatical leaves and travel assistance for professional meetings. The attitude of administrative support was reflected in the president's statement that "from the point of view of the administration these are the most cost effective dollars we have." It was his belief that these expenditures would have a major positive effect on the educational program of the college and provide the ability to adapt to future needs and changes.

But administrative support means much more than budgetary commitments. In fact, the non-financial manifestations of administrative backing for renewal of teacher-scholars may be just as important, if not more important.

Interviews with faculty in the twenty colleges indicated that one of the most important signs of administrative support is simply showing genuine interest in faculty members' development. Time and again I interviewed faculty members who expressed thanks and excitement that someone was taking time to talk with them about their scholarly projects or teaching ideas. They explained that no administrator on their own campus had done so, not even in relation to activities for which they had received college faculty development funds. An administrator's personal interest and backing can be an important stimulus to a faculty member's professional contributions and continuing renewal.

Administrators can also assist renewal efforts by maintaining an open mind to new ideas. A faculty member at one campus described the atmosphere for renewal as follows: "If someone here says 'I've got a great idea!' he or she will get support from administrators and colleagues. This is a place that welcomes new ideas." Administrators may not in the long run be able to back each idea for reasons of financial or sound academic planning, but being willing at least to listen creates a climate for renewal.

Administrative support also means sending out clearer signals to faculty as to what is expected of them. Faculty often reported their sense of frustration from confusing signals as to the importance of scholarship, teaching, and faculty development on their campuses. On the other hand on campuses where a vigorous faculty development program was conducted alongside higher standards and clearer expectations for professional development, faculty often responded positively and enthusiastically, stating expectations in relation to interdisciplinary work is especially important, for faculty need strong administrative support to offset the natural tendencies of department heads oriented to their disciplines. A faculty member cannot make any long-term commitment to broader interdisciplinary learning unless his or her work will be given equal credit to that of discipline-oriented teacher-scholars.

An active faculty development program with funds substantial enough to support a variety of faculty and projects provides administrators with another important lever, namely, accountability. This means that administrators must carefully keep track of faculty projects and not be afraid to gently but firmly point out deficiencies or unfulfilled promises. Likewise, administrators must conscientiously reward faculty—by praise, encouragement, and further financial backing—who take seriously the call for continuing professional renewal.

Another key aspect of administrative support is ensuring that faculty development programs are well managed. This means carefully overseeing the program, getting respected faculty involved, listening to their advice, and communicating both the opportunities for renewal and the results of renewal activities to all faculty on campus. As stressed in an earlier chapter, all the interviewers who assisted in the AAC Project agreed that good program management was a key to success in faculty development.

Administrators must also be prepared to take an active leadership role in areas where faculty are less likely to do so. A friend once told me the apocryphal story of a tombstone in Arizona with the following words printed on it: "See, I told you I was sick." There are several areas where faculty are not ordinarily going to take the lead in admitting deficiencies and needs in saying, "See, I told you." One such sensitive area is teaching improvement. Programs focusing on teaching practices must usually be initiated by administrators, who hopefully can enlist the aid of a few key faculty. Likewise corporate faculty renewal activities, and especially those which stretch across disciplines often demand administrative encouragement. Faculty more naturally follow the lead of their own departments and sometimes need another strong force to begin to think about interrelationships.

Thus, administrators must not be hesitant about being more directive at times. One administrator finally realized this when he observed in an interview that faculty development funds on his campus had been used "more responsively than provocatively" and he intended to shift the emphasis in the future.

Finally, administrators must not only take leadership to make faculty development work, they must also know when to get out of the way.

Sometimes faculty are reluctant to get involved in teaching improvement efforts (which implicitly recognize deficiencies) if they feel they are being watched too closely by administrators who must make judgments on their work for purposes of reappointment, salary adjustments or promotion. Without giving up fiscal and leadership responsibilities, administrators can at times grant enough leeway to faculty committees so that faculty have a genuine sense of "ownership" of the faculty renewal program.

One college president spoke of the need on his campus to "create an atmosphere of enthusiasm for what we are doing." An active faculty development program can assist greatly in creating such an atmosphere, but strong administrative support and sensitive leadership is absolutely necessary if the program is to succeed.

Chapter 13

Colleagueship Among Faculty:
The Challenge of Tolerance

In Hawthorne's novel *The House of the Seven Gables,* there is a scene where the joyful Phoebe walks into the long-neglected garden near the house. Hawthorne's well-chosen words describe the garden's condition as follows: "Besides the rosebush, she had observed several other species of flowers growing there in a wilderness of neglect, and obstructing one another's development (as is often the parallel case in human society) by their uneducated entanglement and confusion."[1]

Just like plants human beings have the proven ability to "obstruct one another's development." Unfortunately the same can be said for many of those human beings who serve as administrators and faculty in our colleges and universities. This is surprising since developing people is what college is all about. Still, obstruction does take place as persons get in each other's way, especially because of intolerant attitudes toward colleagues. The interviews conducted on the twenty campuses were generally very pleasant experiences. One exception was the unpleasantness of hearing the number of times faculty members were too quick to criticize their colleagues in an unhealthy fashion that surely would not promote one another's development.

Just as the previous chapter was directed primarily at administrators, this one is aimed primarily at faculty. As one faculty observer remarked, "The natural tendency of faculty is to be intellectually critical." It is therefore often hard for them to affirm or support their colleagues. Veblen perhaps expressed it best when he said: "Faculty are persons who think otherwise."

One particular interview finally prompted me to write this chapter, for it pointed out so painfully well the intolerant attitude I had encountered too often. This particular faculty member began by criticizing harshly the members of the Faculty Research Committee who were in charge of recommending small study grants on his campus. In the eyes of this faculty member they were "completely lacking in expertise" for their job. It was later I learned that two members of this person's department had been denied grants by the Committee. Lack of expertise in this case meant lack of agreement with his point of view. Concerning the college's Committee on Teaching this same faculty member remarked, "It's a tar baby. What could they talk about?"

This tendency to attempt to build oneself up by putting someone else down or to quickly criticize an idea or program before trying to understand it appeared more often than was comfortable throughout the interviews. This unhealthy intolerance toward others' opinions and actions is perhaps the most disheartening manifestation of the decline in colleagueship. In essence what the faculty member who favors a single, narrow model of teaching or scholarship (or faculty behavior in general) is saying, is that "all faculty should be like me," rather than recognizing the potentially rich diversity of professional contributions, all within the model of the teacher-scholar.

What does this attitude of intolerance have to do with faculty development? Simply this. It is a key factor in "obstructing" the development of faculty colleagues. Many faculty will be left out of development programs which are conceived too narrowly by a small group of like-minded persons. Such was the case with many faculty who testified in interviews that they would not apply for renewal support because the faculty development committee supported only certain kinds of research or teaching. One faculty member, for example, spoke enthusiastically about his research ideas in government but became very despondent when the conversation turned to gaining support from his colleagues for "non-empirical" research differing from their approach. Another faculty member wanted to try out several new ideas in teaching but finally decided not to, because he simply did not want to face the non-supportive criticism of his colleagues.

Renewal of a sense of colleagueship will be vitally important to colleges in the coming critical years. If good morale is to be retained or restored on college campuses, not only administrators, but also faculty must provide a supportive atmosphere for each other.

During times of retrenchment—which many colleges will face—there will be a need for some faculty to move to different substantive areas of teaching in order to fill in curricular gaps. This move may mean that certain faculty will be teaching courses they have not taught for a long time or perhaps have never taught. In the few campuses where such shifts had already taken place, those faculty called upon to tackle these new assignments usually did so very willingly. In fact, many saw it as an opportunity to take on something new and exciting—a truly "renewing" adventure. However, they sometimes ran into real roadblocks from colleagues in their own or in other departments who saw them as "not qualified" or worried that they were infringing on someone else's territory. Even in more normal times—when retrenchment is not the order of the day—faculty who gain new interests because of active renewal programs often run into the same roadblocks. But in years ahead faculty will have to move from a defensive, "gate-keeping" posture to support and even encouragement for colleagues willing to take on important new assignments.

Attitudes of intolerance or indifference toward faculty colleagues remove one of the most important motivating factors for faculty renewal, namely, peer support. During the on-campus interviews faculty members spoke very appreciatively of colleagues who showed interest in what they were doing in research or teaching. They saw this type of support as a special sign that their work was worthwhile and were encouraged to work harder. On the other hand many faculty voiced feelings of real isolation, as they pointed out that they had "never heard from a colleague" about their work in either research or the classroom.

For those who are in charge of faculty development programs another kind of tolerance must be emphasized, namely, tolerance toward those who do not take part in the formal renewal program, often for some very legitimate reasons. To be sure some faculty do not enter into formal campus renewal activities because of personal uncertainties and fears, resistance to the unfamiliar, or simple apathy. But others do not always require formal college support for these renewal activities. At each campus I always asked to interview several faculty who had not participated in the college's faculty development program. In interviewing one such faculty member I was surprised to discover that he had not applied for a research grant and had not attended the faculty teaching seminars, not because he was afraid or resistant, but because he was quite self-reliant. He was an active researcher and writer, had virtually no equipment or travel support needs, and was highly motivated toward self-renewal. Not every faculty member requires our formal, competitive programs and structures.

All of the colleges I visited as part of the AAC Project on Faculty Development were liberal arts colleges. As such they prided themselves on teaching tolerance toward others' opinions, ideas, beliefs and cultures as a key element in liberal learning. How ironic that we must remind faculty of this same teaching in regard to relations with their faculty colleagues.

Periodic reminders to faculty will not be enough to reduce intolerance and indifference in favor of encouragement and support. However, there were signs during the campus visits that one of the best ways to counter such attitudes is with a vigorous program of faculty development, especially one which provides opportunities for both individual and corporate renewal and is flexible enough to meet a variety of needs. For example, one faculty member perceived that the active program of grants for professional development and retooling on his campus had made "faculty realize that change was indeed possible." At another campus a faculty member spoke of his new appreciation for faculty development because of his feeling that many of his colleagues "had gained much" from participation in the on-campus program. Other faculty, as reported in an earlier chapter, emphasized the new, more positive attitudes toward their colleagues acquired through participation in group renewal activities. Finally, others indicated that the renewal program had "set new standards for everybody," including enough diversity within those standards to encourage teacher-scholars to be recognized by their colleagues for various types of renewal achievements.

It should be emphasized that while lack of tolerance is a major obstacle which often stands in the way of a supportive renewal atmosphere, there were many faculty who demonstrated strong support for their colleagues, even when their activities differed in either substance or technique. This highly tolerant attitude was epitomized by a chemistry professor at one college who remarked, "I thought that interdisciplinary symposium was a good idea, even though I knew I couldn't personally get involved with it." The type of teacher-scholar who will be most helpful in college renewal efforts is the one who knows the difference between backbiting, jealous criticism and intellectually honest criticism and who will lend support either by joining in or voicing encouragement from the sidelines even when the activity is not his or her cup of tea.

[1]Nathaniel Hawthorne, *The House of the Seven Gables* (New York: New American Library, 1961), p. 69.

Chapter 14

The Challenge of Commitment: Individual and Institutional

Where Should Loyalty Lie?

One of the great strengths of the liberal arts college has been a committed faculty, committed not only to good teaching and solid scholarship but also to the welfare of the institution in which they were serving. There are disturbing signs, however, that this institutional loyalty has been severely weakened in recent years. At one of the colleges in the AAC study, a senior faculty member said of his colleagues, "There is too damn little enthusiasm for the institution you are working for these days."

Throughout our interviews faculty members demonstrated a confusion of loyalty. Forces, many seemingly beyond their control, keep pulling them in various directions so that it is hard to decide where loyalty and commitment should lie.

We have spoken of various points in this volume of the pull of the disciplines. Faculty often seek to gain a sense of direction and recognition from their disciplinary professions. Consequently, they think of themselves first as biologists, political scientists, sociologists, etc., and only secondarily as a member of a particular faculty. Serving one's "profession" in this more narrow sense has its benefits, of course, for both the individual and higher education generally, but it can lead to isolation from both colleagues and issues of great importance to the local institution.

It is hard to be loyal to an institution in which you do not feel a part of a meaningful community. In many of our institutions we unfortunately may be past the point of speaking of maintaining "community" in the older sense of a group of persons dedicated to a common goal and strongly supportive of each other in that dedication. Still there are qualities associated with community that can be recaptured, especially in smaller liberal arts colleges—collegiality, participation, communication, fairness, and trust. We have documented earlier the deeper concerns of faculty members which are tied to faculty renewal issues—poor communication between departments and divisions; lack of support from colleagues and administrators in relation to their particular interests; mistrust of the decision-making process especially in relation to personnel issues. As a result of these gaps in corporate support we seem to have replaced a sense of community with a purely legislative system of relating to each other, with more and more being written down in larger and larger faculty and staff handbooks. It is hard to hold a sense of loyalty to a set of legal documents.

Economic pressures have also made institutional loyalty more difficult. Colleges have struggled to try to keep faculty salary increases in line with inflation, but many faculty have felt that their financial needs were not being given high enough priority by the college or by the society in general. A direct strain on institutional loyalty has been caused by faculty seeking additional work outside the college in order to increase income. In certain cases outside consulting or part-time employment can assist scholarship and teaching where it is directly related, but in other cases it can hinder teaching, research, and college commitments.

Alternative Careers for the Teacher-Scholar?

In recent years another approach to faculty renewal has arisen which could either assist the faculty member in deciding where his or her loyalties should lie or could add to the confusion. Stimulated by the writings of Sheehey, Levinson, and others focusing on adult development and by the tightened market for faculty positions, some leaders in higher education have been encouraging the creation of programs which allow faculty to examine and explore alternative careers.

Two of the most comprehensive programs are found in the Pacific Northwest. The University of Puget Sound has a program which includes career counseling for faculty, placement assistance, workshops in career planning, a summer course in business skills, and internships in businesses, government and social agencies. In conjunction with the Council of Independent Colleges, the Associated Schools of the Pacific Northwest operates workshops on life and career planning and assists individual faculty interested in exploring new options.

One of the dangers of such programs is that faculty will see the objective as essentially "outplacement" from the college, rather than as assistance for examining their broader life goals, including their teaching and scholarship goals within the college setting. If faculty perceive that the college is encouraging alternative careers as a way of solving tenure and staffing problems, their own sense of institutional interest and loyalty will obviously be negatively affected. It is interesting to note that in reaction to expressed faculty concerns the CIC-ASPN group changed the name of their program from "Alternative Careers," to a program "In Support of Career Planning and Development."

Another danger in such programs is that we may, through seminars, internships, and placement lose some of our best people from the academy. Those who are good at teaching and scholarship often tend to be the most aggressive in responding to new opportunities. Experiences thus far seem to indicate that though this danger is real, it may be overstated, especially where the college maintains at the same time a supportive, comprehensive faculty development program for its teacher-scholars. Leaders in the Pacific Northwest programs indicate that while some faculty will be stimulated to explore seriously alternative careers outside the academy, others will emerge from the program having reaffirmed their commitment to being teacher-scholars. It is clear that such programs must be accompanied by sensitive individual counseling by deans and department chairpersons, encouraging certain faculty to explore alternative careers, while at the same time giving vigorous support for teaching and scholarship on the campus. In this way faculty will recognize that the college does care about individual satisfaction and career development, while at the same time it intends to do all it can to keep and support its dedicated teacher-scholars. The result for many faculty may be a strengthening of loyalty to teaching, scholarship and the college itself.

Individual Loyalty and Institutional Support

What does all this concern about loyalty have to do with faculty renewal? Simply this. A strong liberal arts college is highly dependent upon the presence of a faculty dedicated to its broader goals. If loyalties lie elsewhere, the college's program and especially its students will begin to suffer. The college's curriculum will not receive the faculty's care and concern and will not be adapted to meet changing needs; faculty will not receive support from colleagues; institutional goals will be stated in catalogues, but not manifested on campus; an active intellectual community will not exist.

But how can faculty loyalty be attained and then maintained? Certainly it cannot be demanded; it must be fostered and developed. First and foremost the college itself must have a clear sense of mission and a well-defined set of goals. It is not possible to be loyal to a set of shifting, whispering objectives. Some liberal arts colleges in recent years, including church-related ones, have moved away from their basic missions, attempting to become all things to all people, becoming so pluralistic that a sense of direction is lost. The result has been the addition of new faculty who have little concern for institutional mission and confusion of purpose for senior faculty. A clear sense of mission and the recruitment and tenuring of faculty who care about that mission will result in a renewed sense of loyalty and dedication. Liberal arts colleges must have people who see their work as not simply a job, but as a vocational commitment.

But the college, no matter how well defined its mission, cannot expect commitments from individual faculty unless it in turn is willing to make certain commitments to them. Providing reasonable salary support is one important sign of commitment. But of equal and perhaps greater importance is the commitment to quality education, good teaching, solid scholarship, and continuing institutional renewal that comes from a comprehensive faculty development program. Faculty are much more likely to remain loyal to an institution which continually calls forth the best in its people, by encouraging them, supporting them, rewarding them in ways detailed in the chapters throughout this book.

Finally, two things must be emphasized. In constructing programs of faculty renewal colleges must remember that faculty members are not all alike. Just like students, they differ in their interests, needs, and degree of openness to learning. That is why this book has emphasized the great importance of a college utilizing to the extent possible a variety of approaches to faculty renewal. Some faculty will respond enthusiastically to new opportunities for scholarly research and study, others will not. Some will eagerly explore new approaches to teaching, others will feel they simply cannot get involved in programs dealing directly with classroom teaching improvement. At times a concentration on curricular renewal may be the best approach to faculty development, at other times organizational changes may be more important. At all times careful attention to the process of renewal is called for, especially questions of purpose, planning, communication, management, and program evaluation. Programs emphasizing individual development must be balanced by corporate renewal activities. In sum, those colleges that are able to put together a multifaceted, flexible approach will be able to affect the professional and personal lives of more faculty and do so with greater impact.

Secondly, colleges must recognize that faculty renewal is not a short-term process. A quick burst of faculty development energy will not have much lasting impact. Programs will have to be created, kept intact, sometimes altered. Emphasis may be needed in one approach for a while, in another area in other years. Institutional commitment will have to be long and sincere, not short and doubtful.

Educational quality in our liberal arts colleges is primarily a function of the individuals who teach there. If we wish to maintain quality, we must commit ourselves to institutionalize effective programs of faculty renewal and faculty support. Faculty in turn must give a large measure of loyalty to the institution in which they serve. If institutions and individuals are committed to each other, then, in spite of the difficult years ahead in American higher education, liberal arts colleges will continue to have a significant impact on our youth and our society in general.

As I finished writing the above words, originally intended to be the last in the book, I began to think: Was it worthwhile? The visits to colleges around the country; the interviews with faculty, administrators, students; the analysis and writing? Would it make any difference? Was there still hope for not only continuing renewal of individual teacher-scholars, but also the teacher-scholar ideal in our colleges, especially as we move into the difficult, threatening years ahead?

The writing of this last chapter took place at Holden Village, a Lutheran retreat center in the Cascades in northern Washington. After completing the chapter and filled with these troublesome questions, I went for a walk along a mountainous road outside the village. Along the way I encountered a geologist whom I had met briefly the day before. During our conversation he mentioned that his research and exploration in the northern Cascades was being supported in part by his small college in central Missouri. He explained that in earlier summers he had worked for an oil company to earn some additional funds, but that there had been a change in the presidency at his college, and funds for some research and travel were now available from the college. "Faculty without opportunities for renewal are dying on the vine," he stated emphatically to me. I uttered some words of agreement, and we continued our walks in different directions. But that amazingly timely conversation in an unlikely place had brought back memories of hundreds of similar exchanges during the campus visits in the AAC study. It had reaffirmed for me that for the sake of both individual and institutional vitality, renewal of the teacher-scholar will always be crucial.

APPENDIX I:

Faculty Development: A Variety of Approaches

The following descriptions discuss briefly various successful approaches to faculty development. While most of these programs were studied in connection with the AAC Project on Faculty Development, other institutions' activities are mentioned as well.

Professional Development
Austin College
Career Development Program

The Austin College Career Development Program grew out of a faculty committee examination of alternatives to tenure. Although tenure has been retained, Austin now requires a five-year career development plan for all faculty and top administrators. Each plan is developed by the individual in consultation with colleagues or a consultant (a retired faculty member) and must be submitted to the divisional dean, provost, and president for approval. A faculty member cannot be considered for tenure, promotion, sabbatical or special individual development grant without a completed professional growth plan. Retention of tenure is conditional upon continued pursuit of the objectives in the growth plan.

Contact:
Dan Bedsole
Vice President for Academic Affairs
Austin College
Sherman, TX 75090
214/892-9101

Beloit College
Small Grant Program for Retraining Faculty

Grants ranging from $150 to $2,000 have been used to assist faculty to retool in certain areas in order that they might teach courses which they had not taught previously or for some time. Retrenchment at Beloit created gaps in the curriculum, requiring new teaching assignments.

Reprinted from *The Forum for Liberal Education*, October 1979.

Most faculty undertook these new assignments willingly and appreciated the grant assistance allowing them to study at appropriate graduate centers. A committee of three faculty members advised the provost in awarding these grants. Examples include a religion professor doing graduate study in world religions, an English professor taking a Chaucer course for the first time in 30 years, a physical chemistry teacher moving into biochemistry and organic chemistry, and an economist undertaking management studies. Ironically, it was the necessity of retrenchment which allowed many of these faculty to move into areas of their extended interests.

Contact:
Zeddie Bowen
Provost
Beloit College
Beloit, WI 53511
608/365-4959

Colgate University
Senior and Junior Faculty Grants

Designed to stimulate new ideas and projects, senior faculty grants allow those faculty to take one semester off to study in unfamiliar areas of their disciplines. While most applications for these grants come from the faculty themselves, some individuals have been encouraged to pursue specific projects. As a result of these leaves, many senior faculty have been revitalized; for example, a religion professor became excited about the study of African Christian theology, while an English professor gained new interest in Asian literature. Some faculty have been able to link these leaves with a regular half-year sabbatical, thereby creating a full-year's leave at full pay.

Junior faculty development grants provide half-year leaves for non-terminal faculty who have successfully stood for a third-year review. Administered by the university's Research Council, the grants encourage junior faculty to start on new research projects beyond their dissertation areas.

Contact:
Dean
Colgate University
Hamilton, NY 13346
315/824-1000

Earlham College
Five-Year Review of Tenured Faculty

In 1975 Earlham inaugurated a required program of a five-year review for its tenured faculty. A three-person faculty committee is selected by the faculty member to be reviewed, who then assembles a dossier that includes a self-evaluation, evaluation forms and letters from present and former students, letters from faculty colleagues, and other relevant documentation. The committee consults with the faculty member before, during, and after the dossier is prepared and then forwards its report to the dean (with a copy to the faculty member). The dean in turn meets with the faculty member to decide ways in which the college can assist in the continued professional growth of the faculty member.

Contact:
Joe Elmore
Provost and Dean of Academic Affairs
Earlham College
Richmond, IN 47374
317/962-6561

Furman University
Mid-Career Faculty Development Grants

This project, supported by funding from the Mellon Foundation, has provided 25 faculty with either full or partial support to supplement sabbatical or regular salaries and enabled them to travel and conduct research. In order to qualify for these funds, faculty must be between the ages of 35 and 55 and have developed a five-year faculty growth plan, which is used as the basis for making the grants. In the first year of the program, 41 faculty applied for funding. Most faculty have found that the growth plan exercise was valuable in itself and recommended that it be done regardless of the availability of funding.

Contact:
John Crabtree
Academic Dean
Furman University
Greenville, SC 29613
803/294-3075

Hope College
Summer Fellowships and Dean's Discretionary Fund

Summer fellowships, with the assistance of outside funding, have provided stipends and expense funds for specific research projects. These awards have stimulated many faculty, especially in the humanities, to begin or return to research projects. As a result, these funds have produced new faculty enthusiasm for their work, more student involvement in research, increased interest in and preparation of outside grant proposals, and additional faculty publications. This type of small grant program, while common among many colleges, is especially noteworthy at Hope because of the careful administration of the program, its clear guidelines, and the reporting of project results back to the entire faculty by the dean and the faculty review committee.

The dean's discretionary fund was made possible by a foundation grant to enable support for faculty needs outside regular categories of funding. Previous uses of the fund have included support for programs, conference fees, speaker fees, publication costs, regular trips to other institutional libraries, acquisition of materials for teaching and research, and workshops on teaching and learning. Faculty have reacted positively to the support obtained from the fund and noted ways in which this has improved the atmosphere on campus for faculty growth.

Contact:
David G. Marker
Provost
Hope College
Holland, MI 49423
616/392-5111

St. Lawrence University
Student Involvement Grants

Students seldom play a direct role in the professional development of faculty. St. Lawrence has a unique approach in which a committee of fifteen students accepts faculty proposals and awards grants approximately $500 in size and totalling $2,000 to $5,000 per year. All funds are raised by the committee, usually from off-campus sources. While the original focus was to provide assistance for pre-tenured, pre-doctoral faculty to complete their Ph.D. dissertations, the grant program has broadened to consider any faculty project that will clearly improve classroom or other teaching performance. The committee receives considerable help from the dean, but otherwise seeks information on grantees from faculty and other students.

Contact:
George H. Gibson
Vice President and Dean
St. Lawrence University
Canton, NY 13617
315/379-5011

Instructional Development
Central Pennsylvania Consortium
New Faculty Institute

For several years this consortium (Franklin and Marshall, Gettysburg, Dickinson, and formerly Wilson College) has provided a four-day institute for new faculty. Ordinarily conducted by an outside consultant, the institute has allowed new faculty to explore the meaning and purpose of teaching and to examine important issues in approaches to classroom teaching. The institute has helped younger faculty make the transition from scholarly, discipline-oriented graduate school programs to college teaching.

Contact:
Beverly Eddy
Director, Central Pennsylvania Consortium
Dickinson College
Carlisle, PA 17013
717/243-5121

Earlham College
The Teaching Consultant

Earlham utilizes a faculty member to serve half time as a teaching consultant for other faculty. The consultant, who is formally appointed by the dean, is selected by a poll of faculty to determine the person they would most trust in this role. The teaching consultant counsels faculty, giving them feedback on individual teaching and professional problems, providing support for faculty trying new teaching ventures, and generally assisting in other ways as needed. The teaching consultant is carefully insulated from the formal evaluation process and may not be a member of the Faculty Affairs Committee until at least three years after completion of the consultancy. During the first three years of this program more than 70 percent of the faculty have benefitted from the services of the teaching consultant.

Contact:
Paul Lacey
Professor of English
Earlham College
Richmond, IN 47374
317/962-6561

Furman University
Experienced Faculty Assisting Younger Faculty

At Furman, a group of experienced faculty members has been serving as in-house consultants for younger faculty on teaching and learning. In the past year these faculty have inaugurated a series of seminars focused on such issues as lecturing, images of good teaching, leading discussions, and learning theory. While aimed at younger faculty, the seminars have attracted a number of senior participants as well. In a related program, Furman is instituting a formal program whereby several experienced teachers and new teachers will work together in a one-to-one, mentor-novice relationship. The two persons will observe one another's classes and share evaluations and ideas for improvement. It is anticipated that not only the novice teacher but also the senior faculty member will grow from this experience.

Contact:
John Crabtree
Academic Dean
Furman University
Greenville, SC 29613
803/294-3075

Gettysburg College
Writing Workshop

More and more colleges are beginning to see the importance of all faculty, not just those in departments of English, participating in the teaching of good writing. A writing workshop at Gettysburg prepared faculty to take on this important responsibility by assisting faculty with their own writing skills and by helping them to evaluate better their student's writing. Led by English professors from the college, the workshop was well attended by members of several different departments.

Contact:
James Pickering
Department of English
Gettysburg College
Gettysburg, PA 17325
717/334-3131

Lawrence University
One-to-One Classroom Teaching Consultant

This effort in faculty development came about almost accidentally. A retired, well-respected professor of theater was asked by the dean of the Music Conservatory to assist him with his style of teaching. The results were so positive that the idea expanded to other faculty in the Conservatory, and then to other departments in the college. The consultant sits in on the classes of individual faculty members for the ten-week term and offers weekly "private lessons." He does not try to demonstrate new teaching techniques, but instead teaches faculty how to present themselves in the classroom, giving attention to voice placement, diction, pitch levels, and overcoming the monotony of their voices. The consultant spots also any lack of preparation and helps faculty review carefully what they have prepared for a particular day. As a result, several members of the faculty (at both junior and senior levels) have become more confident about their teaching.

Contact:
Richard Warch
President
Lawrence University
Appleton, WI 54911
414/739-3681

Pomona College
Computer Workshop

Many faculty, particularly those in the humanities, have had little if any experience in the use of computers as research and instructional aids. When its faculty became aware of the usefulness of computers for these purposes, Pomona introduced a computer workshop to enable faculty to gain hands-on experience with computers and to realize the potential for use in instruction. The workshop, conducted by a professor of geology and a consultant from IBM, met once each week during the semester. In addition, faculty were given opportunities for individual assistance to gain facility with a computer.

Contact:
Donald B. McIntyre
Chairman, Department of Geology
Pomona College
Claremont, CA 91711
714/621-8000

Curriculum Change
Berea College
Summer Seminars and Study Grants
for Interdisciplinary Teaching

Seminars, usually two weeks in length, have been conducted over the past four summers to improve faculty competence in areas outside their disciplines, particularly in support of four core courses: "Issues and Values," "Religions and Historical Perspectives," "Man and the Arts," and "Christian Faith in the Modern World." The seminars involved outside experts and facilitators, although the "Man and the Arts" seminar used only on-campus resources. The seminars were judged by most people to be successful in helping faculty gain new confidence and to overcome the apprehension of tackling new material.

Berea has also received foundation funds to support faculty half-year leaves for study in areas outside their regular disciplines as preparation for teaching in interdisciplinary programs. While this approach is more costly than on-campus development programs, these leaves have been successful because they are tied to the faculty members returning to teach specific interdisciplinary courses in the core curriculum.

Contact:
William Stolte
Dean of the College
Berea College
Berea, KY 40404
606/986-9341

Bowdoin College
Grants for Course Development

These grants have supported faculty members seeking to develop new, less traditional courses for the Bowdoin curriculum or to make significant changes in existing courses. Most of the funds have been used for travel expenses or for purchase of supporting material for the courses.

Courses that have been developed include "Women in the Americas," which compares women in Latin America and the United States, and "Mythologies of Europe." Several faculty have indicated that these new courses would not have been developed without the stimulation of the specific grants.

Contact:
Alfred H. Fuchs
Dean of the Faculty
Bowdoin College
Brunswick, ME 04011
207/725-8731

Haverford College
Interdisciplinary Course Development

A number of interdisciplinary courses have been developed through the merger of two existing courses. As a new approach to the development of these courses, faculty from the existing courses attend each other's classes in order to understand the perspective each brings to the subject matter. These faculty then work together to develop an interdisciplinary syllabus that will best complement the major points from the two courses. An additional benefit to this approach has been the insights gained by some faculty through observation of their colleagues' classes.

Contact:
Thomas D'Andrea
Provost and Dean of the Faculty
Haverford College
Haverford, PA 19041
215/649-9600

Hope College
Summer Workshops for Senior Seminar Faculty

These workshops have brought together faculty involved in the Hope Senior Seminar, a course which merges questions of faith and learning. The workshops are four to five weeks in length, and utilize both outside resource persons in theology, ethics, and values, and local resources to encourage faculty to integrate faith and learning and to prepare them to handle questions of faith and ethics in relation to their own disciplines. As at other colleges with similar group experiences, important side benefits were noted: the excitement of interdisciplinary dialogue, the increase in collegiality, a new openness and trust among faculty, and the recruitment of new faculty leadership for the seminar.

Contact:
David Marker
Provost
Hope College
Holland, MI 49423
616/392-5111

Organizational Change
Colgate University
Faculty Development Council

Created to oversee the implementation of a foundation grant, the faculty development council is composed of eight faculty appointed by the dean. With an annual budget of approximately $15,000, the council has awarded small grants to faculty for the improvement of teaching. While the council originally saw its role as one of working with faculty and their ideas to improve teaching and revitalize the curriculum, the small number of faculty proposals prompted the council to take a stronger role by sponsoring workshops and inviting specific proposals for interdisciplinary curriculum development. Examples of these projects include the development of courses on women's studies, the integration of sciences and humanities, and Colgate University as an institution.

Contact:
Anthony Aveni
Chairman, Faculty Development Council
Colgate University
Hamilton, NY 13346
315/824-1000

Kenyon College
Summer Seminars for Faculty

The Kenyon seminars are intensive, two-week investigations of the liberal arts at the college, designed to overcome faculty compartmentalization and division. During the first two years in which they were held, the seminars focused on Kenyon's philosophy of education, the role of the faculty in providing that education, and the needs of the students.

In the past two years the focus has shifted from "talking about" the liberal arts to concentrating on substantive issues of broad inter-disciplinary interest. Three faculty members lead the seminars; nearly 80 percent of Kenyon's faculty have participated in the seminars since they began. As a result, faculty have noted greater individual scholarly development and increased appreciation for their colleagues.

Contact:
Provost
Kenyon College
Gambier, OH 43022
614/427-2244

St. Lawrence University
The Academic Resources Board

The academic resources board, composed of nine present faculty members appointed by the president and chaired by a retired faculty member, is responsible for defining and carrying out faculty develop-ment programs at the university. Through a careful process of ex-perimentation and evaluation (supported by a series of small grants), the board has created a more receptive attitude on campus for faculty development. At the end of this process the board produced a "Systematic Plan for Faculty Renewal," a report setting forth long-term priorities for faculty development.

Contact:
Alfred Romer
Department of Physics
St. Lawrence University
Canton, NY 13617
315/379-5011

APPENDIX II:

Faculty Development: Resources
(compiled by Michael E. Siegel)

> *Faculty development is a multi-facted human phenomenon. As such, it encompasses the professional growth of faculty, the improvement of their pedagogy, as well as their striving to fashion curricular changes and organizational improvements. It also relates to their growth and development as human beings, to the struggles they experience and the hopes that they have. There is no one correct or foolproof approach to faculty development. Accordingly, the literature suggested here reflects different dimensions of faculty development, cast in a flexible and absorbent conceptual mold.*

Faculty Development: The Context

Freedman, Mervin, ed. "Facilitating Faculty Development." *New Directions in Higher Education.* San Francisco: Jossey-Bass, Vol. 1, 1973.

These essays are based on a study of faculty growth and development sponsored by the Wright Institute, with assistance from the U.S. Office of Education. The researchers interviewed over five hundred faculty members from diverse campuses throughout the country, to ascertain how faculty perceived their own professional careers and developmental needs. In a cogent introductory chapter, the authors note the ambiguity and confusion attached to the contemporary faculty member's role, compared to the "well-trodden" paths and signposts that formerly directed his or her professional ways. Essays that follow address themselves to the need for faculty to carve out a professional identity which is sensitive to change, but also rooted in the faculty member's socialization experiences and personal strengths. The importance of individual differences among faculty is clearly illustrated in one chapter describing faculty conceptions of the teaching art and in another depicting the different reactions of faculty to nontraditional students. As well, one chapter outlines various "stages" of faculty development, and draws some very interesting parallels to the "stages" of student development discovered by William Perry and his colleagues at Harvard. Finally, the concluding essays tackle the question of how to go about faculty development.

Reprinted (with additions) from *The Forum for Liberal Education,* October 1979.

Gardner, John. *Self-Renewal: The Individual and the Innovative Society.* New York: Harper Colophon Books, 1965.

Gardner stresses the importance of self-renewal for all segments of society. As institutions and organizations age, they lose their original sense of vitality and exhibit increasing tendencies of rigidity. Individuals within organizations also display tendencies to stagnate. Consequently, Gardner says, we must design our institutions and our organizations in ways which will encourage individual renewal: "the development of skills, attitudes, habits of mind and the kinds of knowledge, understanding, and insight that will be the instruments of continuous growth."

Group for Human Development in Higher Education. *Faculty Development in a Time of Retrenchment.* New Rochelle: Change Magazine Press, 1974.

The title of this publication suggests its major concern: during an era of "retrenchment" in higher education—when funds become scarce, enrollments shrink, and faculty mobility all but disappears—neglect of faculty development could be disastrous. The authors target most of their comments at the teaching component of faculty development, and lament the absence of training programs for excellent teachers in higher education. Acknowledging the seriousness of the problem, they nonetheless offer various suggestions to improve faculty performance in teaching: special graduate degrees for teaching, teaching improvement centers, teaching workshops, and teaching evaluation methods. One of the more interesting suggestions they make is for graduate schools to broaden the traditional notion of what counts as an original contribution to knowledge. They add: "Neglect and distortion of undergraduate teaching are caused not so much by the widespread emphasis on research as by the narrowing of research rewards to what can most easily be published in disciplinary journals."

Faculty Development: The Need

Hodgkinson, H.L. "Adult Development: Implications for Faculty and Administrators." *Educational Record*, 55, (Fall, 1974).

Hodgkinson utilizes the growing literature on adult development, including the work of Daniel Levinson and Gail Sheehy, to describe the needs of faculty during different phases of their careers. Concepts such as the Dream, the Mentor, "Catch 30," becoming one's own man, middlescence, and restabilization are related to how faculty and administrators view and actualize themselves in their professional roles and the conflicts and crises they have at various stages of their professional lives. His ideas suggest that faculty development focus not only on *programs*, but also on *people*.

Wheeler, Burton M. "Hope and Despair in the Academy," *The Chronicle of Higher Education*, May 15, 1978.

Wheeler laments the despair that has set in among many faculty members and urges them instead to project a sense of hope to their students. He enumerates the reasons for faculty despair, stressing the particular problem of a gulf between faculty and student cultures. Nonetheless, he charges faculty to overcome despair, and avers that it is primarily faculty who are responsible for establishing the ambience of the university.

Light, Donald. "Thinking About Faculty." *Daedalus*, 103, (Fall, 1974).

According to Light, only about 20 percent of faculty members in the U.S. regularly publish articles or books. Thus, by our very rigid and narrow standards only about 20 percent of faculty are "successful." Light urges that we evolve a more flexible conceptualization of success in academia, and provide at least as many paths to distinction as exist, for example, in the legal profession. He notes poignantly that most faculty would like to spend more time on teaching-related activities, but are prevented from doing so by the existing reward structures in many universities and colleges. Thus, faculty development programs ought to focus on methods of expanding the academy's definition of success.

Faculty Development: The Range

Bergquist, W.H. and Phillips, S.R., "Components of an Effective Faculty Development Program." *Journal of Higher Education*, 46, (March/April 1975).

According to the authors the most widely used past approaches to faculty development—reduction of student/faculty ratios, the purchase of instructional equipment, and the recruitment of new Ph.D.'s with supposedly fresh ideas—are no longer adequate to meet the challenges of our times. They advocate a comprehensive approach to faculty development, embracing personal, instructional and organizational development. Their model assumes that changes must occur at the levels of attitude, process, and structure.

Centra, John A. *Faculty Development Practices in U.S. Colleges and Universities*. Princeton: Educational Testing Service, 1976.

This report of a national survey of faculty development activities contains information about frequency and effectiveness of various practices, the extent to which faculty are involved, and the organization and funding of programs. Centra reports that about half the institutions have faculty development activities, that the average age of such programs is a little over two years, and the faculty most actively involved are good teachers who want to improve.

Gaff, Jerry C. *Toward Faculty Renewal: Advances in Faculty, Instructional, and Organizational Development*. San Francisco: Jossey-Bass, 1975.

Gaff defines faculty development as "enhancing the talents, expanding the interests, improving the competence, and otherwise facilitating the professional and personal growth of faculty members, particularly in their roles as instructors." He isolates three different dimensions of faculty renewal: 1) faculty development, including expanding the range of faculty knowledge in terms of subject matter, improving faculty knowledge about higher education, attending to the effective needs of faculty, and expanding faculty knowledge about student development; 2) instructional development, including utilizing innovations and pedagogical approaches, and applying known principles of learning theory to classroom instruction; 3) organizational development, implying that faculty get more involved with the total institution. Gaff reviews many of the programs in faculty development and provides a good list of the major centers of activity throughout the country.

Nelsen, William C. and Siegel, Michael E., ed. *Effective Approaches to Faculty Development*. Washington: Association of American Colleges, 1980.

This book summarizes the major findings of the Association of American Colleges' Project on Faculty Development. That project entailed visits to 20 leading liberal arts colleges to assess the impact of faculty development on these campuses. At each campus extensive interviews were conducted with faculty, administrators and, in some cases, students. It includes essays from faculty and administrators who have been directly involved in demonstrably exciting and effective programs in faculty development on their own campuses. It also includes essays from faculty whose careers have been enhanced by their faculty development activities, and who have been willing to share their feelings on renewal and revitalization with others. The editors also present their own analytical essays which focus on factors that correlate with successful faculty development efforts.

Faculty Development: The How

Bergquist, William H. and Phillips, Steve R. *A Handbook for Faculty Development.* Vol. 1. Washington: Council for the Advancement of Small Colleges, 1975. Vol. II, 1977, Vol. III, 1981.

In these three volumes Bergquist and Phillips describe activities that have been used for instructional, organizational, and personal development. They provide useful exercises for those interested in starting faculty development programs, and for those interested in improving their own teaching performance. As well, they provide good bibliographic information for different aspects of faculty development.

Gaff, Jerry G., ed. "Institutional Renewal Through the Improvement of Teaching." *New Directions in Higher Education.* Vol. 6. San Francisco: Jossey-Bass, 1978.

This is a concise report on the Project on Institutional Renewal Through the Improvement of Teaching (PIRIT), a three-year effort which involved sixteen colleges and universities in a common search for ways to improve teaching and revitalize institutions. This volume includes reports from on-campus PIRIT project directors at a medium-sized university, a large university, and a small liberal arts college. The final four chapters include a discussion by Gaff on how to overcome faculty resistance, a discussion of involving students in faculty development (an often overlooked consideration), and a very useful tabulation of the benefits of faculty members as seen by faculty involved in the PIRIT programs.

Gaff, Sally Shake; Festa, Conrad; and Gaff, Jerry G. *Professional Development: A Guide to Resources.* New Rochelle: Change Magazine Press, 1978.

According to the authors, it often comes as a surprise to faculty members to discover that there is a professional literature on higher education. Since most academics are never exposed to this body of knowledge, the authors have provided an accessible, inexpensive resource containing published materials and resource organization on professional development in academia. Each chapter begins with a brief essay which gives perspective on the given topic (i.e., Faculty and Teaching, Students and Learning, Course Development), raises key issues, identifies major trends, and concludes with a comprehensive, annotated bibliography on that same topic.

Lindquist, Jack, ed. *Designing Teaching Improvement Programs*. Washington: Council for the Advancement of Small Colleges, 1979.

Lindquist provides summaries of ten different approaches to faculty development; for each approach he charts accompanying teaching improvement objectives along with specific activities relevant to the accomplishment of those objectives. Chapters include a review of the literature on the teaching-learning process, and discussions of faculty development at the liberal arts college level, the role of the university center in faculty development, staff development for community colleges, faculty development in the nontraditional setting, and professional development in the inter-institutional setting.

Nelsen, William C. "Faculty Development: Prospects and Potential for the 1980s." *Liberal Education*, 65, (Summer, 1979).

Noting that faculty development will continue to assume a very prominent position on the agenda of colleges and universities during the 1980's, Nelsen makes six suggestions for faculty and administration. The suggestions emerge from a close examination of thirty-three faculty development programs, from a review of the literature, from on-site observations, and from "hardnosed experiences of six years as an academic dean." The suggestions are as follows: 1) faculty development programs must be flexible and sensitive to the individual differences among faculty; 2) individual approaches; however, must be balanced by corporate or collegial activity which takes into account broader institutional goals; 3) the definition of scholarship must be expanded to facilitate intellectual contributions from a wide range of faculty members to the broader academic community; 4) personnel management techniques at the academy must be improved; 5) faculty should familiarize themselves—or be encouraged to do so—with the burgeoning and important literature on student development; 6) administrators must take a strong leadership role in faculty development.

Additional Resources

Exchange. Center for Faculty Evaluation and Development in Higher Education, Kansas State University

This is a quarterly newsletter which contains short descriptions about the Center's own activities, it being one of the most active centers for the promotion of effective faculty evaluation procedures. *Exchange* usually contains valuable reviews of books on faculty development, as well as announcements about upcoming activities and conferences related to faculty development.

Contact:
Exchange
Center for Faculty Evaluation and Development in Higher Education
1617 Anderson Avenue
Box 3000
Manhattan, KS 66502

Faculty Development and Evaluation in Higher Education

A quarterly newspaper which reports on both empirical and experiential studies on faculty development. Frequently, program directors reflect on specific aspects of local faculty development programs. As well, there are articles related to themes in faculty development, such as evaluation techniques, fellowship programs for faculty, student development, and faculty advising. The newspaper also advertises important upcoming conferences related to faculty development.

Contact:
Dr. Albert B. Smith
Editor
Faculty Development and Evaluation Newspaper
3930 N.W. 35th Place
Gainesville, FL 32605

Improving University Teaching

There have now been five international conferences on Improving University Teaching. For each conference, over two hundred papers were prepared by educators throughout the world. Many of the papers deal with the specific issue of faculty development from an international perspective. One can read about faculty evaluation problems in England, a new faculty development program in Hong Kong, resistance to faculty development in Brazil, faculty plans in Canada and many other interesting articles as well. Many of the contributors are Americans; they typically write in an applied, non-theoretical fashion about the process of faculty development in American colleges and universities.

Contact:
Dr. Benjamin Massey
Improving University Teaching
University of Maryland University College
University Boulevard at Adelphi Road
College Park, MD 20742

Professional and Organizational Network in Higher Education

This is a professional association of people who share a commitment to improving higher education. Typically, they are engaged in faculty, administrative, instructional, or organizational efforts. Members share the belief that the teaching-learning process and institutional life in general are strengthened as opportunities for professional and personal grants are opened up to all members of the higher education community. POD currently offers an array of activities, including an annual conference, a quarterly newsletter, and national and regional training workshops.

Contact:
Lance Buhl
Executive Director, POD
1836 Euclid Avenue, Suite 203
Cleveland, OH 44115

aac

Association of American Colleges

1818 R Street, N.W., Washington, D.C. 20009

202/387-3760

March 15, 1982

Dear Colleague:

It is a pleasure for me to send you this copy of <u>Renewal of the Teacher-Scholar</u>, by William C. Nelsen. As you may recall, Dr. Nelsen served as director of AAC's Project on Faculty Development (funded by The Andrew W. Mellon Foundation) in 1979. This book is based on his own observations and conversations with over five hundred faculty, administrators, and students at institutions that participated in that project. <u>Renewal of the Teacher-Scholar</u> examines the current status of the teacher-scholar model, and addresses those issues which are important for institutions designing and implementing effective faculty development programs. It is a reflective, informative, and challenging book that will be of interest to you and your colleagues.

Sincerely yours,

Mark H. Curtis
President

82:8

The National Association for Liberal Learning